A Silk Road
PILGRIMAGE

A Silk Road
PILGRIMAGE

Discovering the Church of the East

Richard and Jewel Showalter

Herald Press
Scottdale, Pennsylvania
Waterloo, Ontario

Library of Congress Cataloging-in-Publication Data

Showalter, Richard.
  A silk road pilgrimage : discovering the church of the East / Richard and Jewel Showalter.
      p. cm.
  Includes bibliographical references.
  ISBN 978-0-8361-9477-7 (pbk. : alk. paper)
  1. Asia–Church history. 2. Christianity–Asia. 3. Silk Road–Description and travel. 4. Christian pilgrims and pilgrimages. I. Showalter, Jewel, 1948- II. Title.
  BR1065.S56 2009
  275.08'3–dc22

                                                    2009012233

A SILK ROAD PILGRIMAGE
Copyright © 2009 by Herald Press, Scottdale, Pa. 15683
  Published simultaneously in Canada by Herald Press,
  Waterloo, Ont. N2L 6H7. All rights reserved
International Standard Book Number: 978-0-8361-9477-7
Library of Congress Catalog Card Number: 2009012233
Printed in the United States of America
Book design by Joshua Byler
Cover by Reuben Graham
Photos supplied by the authors

14 13 12 11 10 09   10 9 8 7 6 5 4 3 2 1

To order or request information please call
1-800-245-7894 or visit www.heraldpress.com.

To Chad and Deborah, Keith and Rhoda, Matthew and Colleen,
our children and fellow pilgrims

Contents

The Silk Road

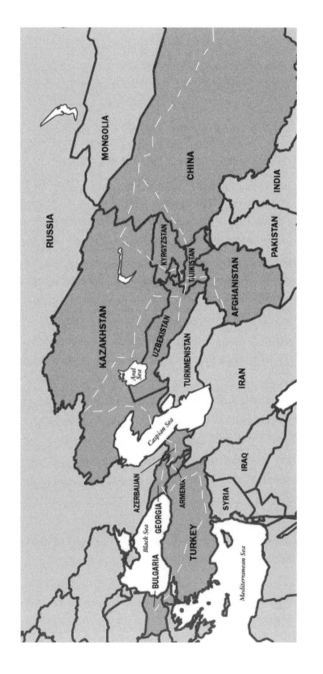

Foreword

It has been said that the history of Christianity, perhaps even western civilization, was transformed in the middle of the first century by God's intervention with a small group of missionaries. Paul and a band of his traveling companions were "kept by the Holy Spirit from preaching the word in the province of Asia" (Acts 16:6). Paul regrouped and again turned his focus eastward toward Bithynia, but "the Spirit of Jesus would not allow them" (Acts 16:7).

The Scripture does not give much detail, but it seems clear that on the heels of these two dramatically closed doors, Paul was seeking further direction. It came in "a vision of a man of Macedonia standing and begging him, 'Come over to Macedonia and help us'" (Acts 16:9). Paul took this vision as clear direction from God and "got ready at once to leave for Macedonia, concluding that God had called us to preach the gospel to them" (Acts 16:10).

As Paul and his missionary band turned toward Macedonia the history of Christianity took on a western flavor. The frontiers of Paul's vision would become Rome and Spain. We can only wonder how differently the history of the church would read if Paul had been allowed to minister in the depths of Asia. What if the vision had been from a man in the Far East, begging Paul for help?

With our attention carried westward by Luke's narrative, who appears to have joined Paul in Troas around the time of his Macedonian vision, "a mist of ignorance," as Richard and Jewel Showalter describe it, rose heavily over the body of Christ that lay east of the Roman empire.

In this carefully documented book, the Showalters shed light on God's work in the East, both in history as well as today, burning away this mist of ignorance. You will be encouraged and informed as you journey with them through trade routes of the ancient Silk Road, celebrating acts of the Holy Spirit as evidenced in the testimonies of God's faithfulness to the church in the east.

Steve Moore
President and CEO
The Mission Exchange

Preface

Nearly five hundred years ago, a small group of Swiss brothers and sisters gathered in the home of Felix Manz on the Neustadtgasse in Zurich and baptized each other from a milk pail. We mark that occasion as the beginning of the Anabaptist movement, the radical wing of the European Reformation.

From that event, and many others like it, the Christian church has been constantly regenerated in mission. The Anabaptists were significant in forming the global evangelical missionary movement of the nineteenth and twentieth centuries, one of many missionary movements throughout history.

We only vaguely perceive many of the complex intersections of Christians in mission because of the mists of our ignorance about the past. Those mists lie particularly heavily over the Church of the East, a far-flung expression of the body of Christ that lay east of the Roman Empire. Roman Catholicism and Eastern Orthodoxy were both expressions of the Christian church inside the Roman Empire, one Latin and the other Greek. These we know best.

East of Roman territory, however, were the ancient Persian, Indian, and Chinese empires, where, during and after the time of the apostles, Syrian and Persian Christians planted far-flung networks of churches that we know as the Church of the East. It flowered for 1400 years until the ravages of the emperor Tamerlane, and its remnants remain today.

The East is where the church experienced one of the longest-lasting, most extensive missionary movements in its history. In October 2007 we set out to explore that movement as we traveled across Asia. What we learned and saw was endlessly thrilling, sobering, and beckoning.

As we traveled, we not only explored the past but also engaged in conversations with missionaries, local church leaders, and residents of the countries we visited.

In these pages we share glimpses of our journey, inviting you to join us in a region of the world that has been traversed for millennia but remains little-known in both the East and the West. Welcome to the journey.

Richard and Jewel Showalter
Landisville, Pennsylvania

Introduction
Our Journey

When we lived and worked in the western Turkic world in the 1980s, our friends often told us proudly that their ancestors had come from central Asia—sweeping down from the steppes into the Byzantine Empire.

In university history-of-civilization classes, we had given scant attention to the great empires of Genghis Khan, Tamerlane, or the Seljuk and Ottoman Turks. Yet these were the glory days that our friends remembered with pride.

The main road through our city was called the Ipek Yolu—the Silk Road—hinting of an exotic past.

But the settled urban communities of Turkey, Bulgaria, and Northern Cyprus, blended as they are with Mediterranean civilizations, seemed far from central Asia. As the Soviet Union's *perestroika* blew new freedoms into the region and gave birth to young central Asian Turkic nations, the region became more accessible to us as westerners.

Several elements converged to spark plans for an overland trip along the ancient trade routes from Xian, China, to Sofia, Bulgaria.

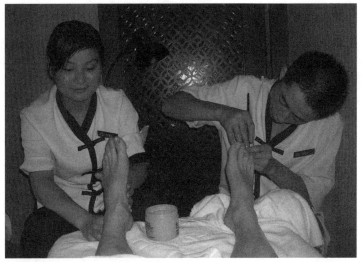

A Chinese foot massage in Shanghai.

One was our longstanding engagement in the Turkic world, which was now more open than ever. There was also Richard's youthful love affair with *Travels of Marco Polo*. Our daughter and her family lived in China, and we had other friends and acquaintances in the region. Then we were privileged to take a three-month sabbatical during our fourteenth year of work at Eastern Mennonite Missions.

Richard's pioneering "follow your nose" instincts and Jewel's more schedule-oriented concern for detail forged an efficient partnership. Between October 7 and December 23, 2007, we walked and biked, boarded hard- and soft-sleeper trains as well as buses, shared taxis, boats, and, yes, even occasionally mounted horses or camels to cover more than ten thousand miles across central Asia.

We had several overarching goals: stay on the ground using the most common means of local transportation, read the history of Christianity in Asia enroute, and pray fervently to see and hear what God is up to in our time.

Our tentative itinerary included a dozen countries. We left the United States with four of the visas we needed, obtaining the last three of these during hurried trips to Washington, D.C. in the final week before departure. The rest we hoped to get along the way.

We got our China visa in Hong Kong, our Uzbek visa in Kazakhstan, but were unable to secure visas in Tashkent for Turkmenistan as we had planned. They would have taken longer to process than we were able to wait. Others we got at border crossings. In another long shot in Tajikistan, we also tried—but failed—to get a visa to Iran. That also would have taken too long.

The Silk Road is not one road, but rather a huge network of trade routes branching and converging across the breadth of Asia, crossing many cultures. With the flexibility of modern travel options, we bounced back and forth among the southern, middle, and northern branches of the trail—now on one, now on another.

Enjoying lunch with Mennonite pastor Jeremiah Choi in Hong Kong.

In China we had help to purchase tickets and negotiate lodging and food from our daughter and her husband, who speak the language of the Middle Kingdom (the Chinese name for China). After entering central Asia, we often wished we knew Russian, the modern imperial language of the region, but we used English and Anatolian Turkish, a central Asian phrase book, translation software on a computer, and pantomimes to communicate our wishes and needs.

The further west we got, the better people understood our form of Turkish, and since the numbers are the same in all the Turkic languages, we could understand "the bottom line" in the bazaar, restaurant, or ticket office.

In central Asia we met two Japanese tourists but not another American. When people learned that we were from the United States, they raised their eyebrows and smiled in a surprised but not unpleasant way. Some told us we were the first Americans they'd ever met, and they thumbed through our passports in curiosity.

People wanted to know how old we were and how much money we made. Many had never heard of our home state, Pennsylvania, but everyone knew of New York, California, and Texas.

After two vodkas too many, a drunken seatmate on the train wanted to show off his knowledge of America. "Schwarzenegger, Arnold Schwarzenegger. Terminator," he slurred and flexed his biceps. From the Chinese border to the Caspian Sea, conversations in trains and taxis led us to believe that Arnold Schwarzenegger, Michael Jackson, and George Bush were the best-known Americans in central Asia. Barack Obama—who's that? We were just ahead of his fame.

And so we returned, not with literal diamonds and rubies sewn into the seams of our clothing as the Polo brothers (Marco's father and uncle) had seven hundred years earlier, but filled with stories, observations, thoughts, and questions. The following chapters are part travelogue, part history, and part reflections on the spread of Christianity in the region.

Today's merchants no longer trade silk, spices, and tea, but oil, gas, carpets, and cotton. In Aktau we met a young woman who works for an American multinational oil company. Another man on the train had a brother who works for the American company Halliburton. Oil is the region's new silk.

But some things don't change. Faithful Christian witnesses continue to trek along these routes, crossing complex national boundries and living precariously. They live and work in the context of falling and rising empires with the news of "a kingdom that cannot be shaken."

Both ancient and modern pilgrims who have passed this way have struggled to translate, contextualize, and incarnate the living

A Kyrgyz woman and child in western China.

Word of God, to live as "lambs among wolves." Their stories amazed and inspired us. They have preached, served, prayed, suffered, and died here. They've seen churches built and demolished. They keep pressing on—part of that kingdom that is quietly filling the whole earth.

Chapter 1

The Ancient Christian Movement in Asia

Around a large, round restaurant table in eastern China, we wielded chopsticks to pick delicious tidbits of food from the rotating Lazy Susan. More fascinating than the gingered green beans or pineapple fish were the stories of the unique group of people assembled to meet us.

One, a former Muslim, now runs a Christian ministry that provides housing and job training for physically handicapped street people. Another, from Southeast Asia, teaches university English, but also runs missionary trainings for house churches. Still another works for a large international business but serves as treasurer for an international fellowship. Also with us was a business consultant who runs team-building workshops for large corporations and also leads Bible studies for maids. She had just helped baptize several new believers.

There was something so robust, authentic, missionary, and truly Christian about the group. And we had the decided impression that this was only a tiny fraction of what these twenty-first-century followers of Jesus were up to.

Marco Polo, a Venetian who spent twenty-six years in Kublai Khan's thirteenth-century China, tells the remarkable story of a group of Christians he discovered in the city of Fu-chau. A learned Muslim companion described a group of people whose religion nobody knew, except that it did not seem to be Buddhist, Muslim, or Christian. Curious, Marco and his uncle went to visit them.

After several days of getting acquainted with the suspicious group, the Venetians learned to their surprise that they were Christians, but that they had been carefully hiding their identity for fear of persecution. They possessed books that turned out to be copies of the Psalms.

When Marco and his uncle asked about the source of their religion, they reported that three of the seventy disciples of Jesus had come to their ancestors long ago and instructed them in the faith. They had since maintained their teaching for many long centuries without further instruction.

With the encouragement of the Venetians, they put in a request and were subsequently recognized as Christians by the court of Kublai Khan. In subsequent research, Marco learned that there were more than seven hundred thousand households of these adherents of ancient Christianity scattered throughout the province.[1]

Western historians, with the characteristic tough-mindedness of their craft, are hard put to explain the story. Were these people really Christians? Were there actually that many of them? Were they remnants of Syrian Christian missions to China from seven hundred years earlier, or did disciples of Jesus actually get that far

The Terra Cotta warriors of Xian, China.

twelve centuries before the Polo brothers arrived in China? Who were the three disciples? No one can answer these questions authoritatively. What we have is a seven-hundred-year-old report, and we can no longer cross-examine Marco or go to his sources. But he is much too reliable a reporter to dismiss out of hand.

There is other evidence for the spread of Christianity eastward—from the Nestorian Tablet and the early Christian training center near Xian to the scrolls of the caves of Dunhuang further west and the more recent excavations in the Chuy Valley at Sujab, east of Bishkek, Kyrgyzstan.[2]

So as we traveled, we read the old story and rejoiced. The good news certainly traveled east along the ancient Asian trade routes beginning in the apostolic era, and for now we must be content with the few glimpses we get from here and there.

∽

Let us fast-forward to the twenty-first century. We had recently seen another Christian mission—a mission to the West, coming from the very lands to which the Syrians and Persians had taken the gospel. Brother Yun, a Chinese house-church leader, was speaking to an international gathering of mission and church leaders in Bechterdissen, Germany, in September 2007. Remembering his months in a maximum-security prison, he recalled saying, "Jesus, I'm in prison." He heard the Lord reply, "I know."

"Those words," Yun said, "have stayed with me for the rest of my life. He knows our weaknesses. I wanted to die for him, but the Lord

showed me he wanted me to live for him. He showed me that he had opened a door that no man could shut. Today I stand to preach because the Lord told me I would preach to the whole world."[3]

We wept as we heard the testimony of this twenty-first-century flame of God from China. He told of his incredible suffering and joy, and the fires of our own passion for Jesus leaped higher toward heaven. He said that the Chinese house-church vision is to take the gospel west-

This pagoda is the only building remaining from the early Syrian-Persian mission to China before the year 1000.

ward, "back to Jerusalem," across the deserts, mountains, oases, and lush river valleys of Eurasia.

It was just one month later that we began our own three-month journey along the ancient trade routes from China, traveling westward back toward Europe.

In Xian and Dunhuang, China, we rode horses or camels for short distances. Later in Kazakhstan and Kyrgyzstan, we saw these animal roaming the wide central Asian plains in great herds. We often walked, sometimes as much as fifteen miles a day. Twice Richard took bike hikes with friends. But mostly we traveled by train, bus, minibus, car, and boat, with one brief round trip by air inside Afghanistan.

The Back to Jerusalem movement of the Chinese house churches is a missionary movement of eastern Christians who are taking the gospel westward along the old Eurasian trade routes. We watched for its signs wherever we went, rejoicing when we found them. This defies the widespread stereotype that Christianity is a western religion carried by European nations.

That stereotype is being shattered, as well it should be. Yet even the best-informed western Christians are only beginning to glimpse how incompletely we have understood the spread of Christianity since Pentecost. For too long we have been ignorant of another ancient missionary movement, the one from Jerusalem eastward, symbolized by Marco Polo's story of the Fu-chau Christians.

The old understandings will not do. Long before western Christian missions to the East (Roman Catholic, Protestant, evangelical) or the newer eastern missions to the west (Korean, Chinese Back to Jerusalem), there was a powerful Christian movement *east to east.*

Paul the apostle, along with many others in the first century, took the good news north and west into Europe by land and sea. That was the first east-to-west missionary movement. It's a story partially told in the New Testament. Informed western Christians know how it continued with the Celtic missionary movement of the British Isles and the evangelization of Europe.

Simultaneously, however, other messengers of Jesus were going east in a movement that was just as powerful and Spirit-anointed as that to the west. The city of Edessa (modern Urfa, Turkey) on the Roman/Persian border became, like Antioch of Syria, an early center of mission. By the fourth century, other centers of Christian mission far to the east had sprung up throughout central Asia, in places like Herat, Balkh, Merv, Bukhara, and Samarkand.[4] Today, however, only a few historians know those stories well.

Furthermore, because the movement was prematurely dismissed as heretical by the early western church and because of the great linguistic and cultural chasms between West and East, the existing documents of that movement have not yet been classified and translated. These documents are scattered in more than fifty libraries and museums in many nations and languages,[5] and one of our reasons for traveling the Silk Road was to reflect on that "hidden" history.[6]

Those early "east to east" missionaries traveled the ancient trade routes eastward, usually by land but sometimes by sea. The routes

The caves of Dunhuang held a treasure trove of ancient manuscripts.

commenced in Constantinople, Antioch, or Tyre on the eastern Mediterranean. They continued across west and central Asia south of the Caspian Sea and across the mountains of modern Kyrgyzstan and Tajikistan, then through far-western China to the ancient Chinese capital at Xian.[7] Other routes crossed the grasslands and deserts north of the central Asian mountains. Still others went south to India, through the mountains from either the west or the east. There were also sea routes to India from both east and west.

The best-known story is that of Thomas the apostle, who traveled east in the first century and has been owned by the resulting Christian communities ever since as the apostle to India.[8] The place of his martyrdom near Madras (Chennai) on the east coast of India is still remembered and revered, and the Syriac churches of South India's Kerala state celebrate an unbroken history back to the first century.

But there were many others besides Thomas who traveled east, though not all of them willingly. For example, the second emperor of the great Sassanid Persian Empire (226-651), Shapur I, captured some Byzantine Roman Christians, including one who had a daughter of such beauty that the fifth Sassanid emperor, Vararhan II (276-293), took her to be a queen.

But when he asked her, "What is your religion?" she replied, "I am a Christian and I serve my Lord Jesus Christ, and I confess God his father."[9] When the Zoroastrian emperor ordered her to abandon her religion and promised that he would then make her the chief queen of the whole realm, she refused to give up her faith. She went to her death "with radiant face," supported by the Christian community.[10]

Amid these challenges the apostles to the east pushed on into central Asia and beyond in a steady stream. A disciple of Addai (one of Jesus' seventy disciples) named Mari had early been sent out from

The sand dunes of Dunhuang on the edge of the formidable Taklamakan Desert—
the nemesis of the Silk Road.

Edessa on a series of difficult missionary journeys that took him almost to India. There he "smelt the smell of the Apostle Thomas" and felt he had gone far enough.[11] These earliest Syrian missionaries were homeless wanderers for Jesus, following the tradition of their master.

Before the end of the second century, Christianity had moved even into the steppes of central Asia to the Turkic tribes along the Oxus (now called Amu Darya) River in the region of modern Mazar-e-Sharif in northern Afghanistan.[12] Here the ancient city of Balkh was soon to become a new center of mission from which missionaries would travel all the way to the imperial courts of the T'ang emperors of China in Xian.[13]

A Sassanid Persian emperor named Shah Kavad (488-497; 501-531) fled to the White Huns north of the Oxus River for refuge after being deposed from the Persian throne for the second time.

With him went two Persian Christians, John of Resh-aina and Thomas the Tanner. For thirty years they lived among the Huns, preaching and baptizing. They reduced their oral language to writing, and taught them to read and write.

Later an Armenian bishop joined them and taught the restless nomads the basic principles of agriculture. The rapid spread of Christianity among the Turkic tribes of central Asia for the next two hundred years can only be explained by the presence this patient, wise, holistic and Christlike witness.[14]

Chapter 2

Creative Access

On the border of China and Kazakhstan, our train stopped in Dostyk, Kazakhstan, for six hours to pass customs and have the bogies (wheels) changed. Train tracks in China are 1.3 meters wide but are 1.5 meters wide in the former Soviet Union. Shyrin, our Kazakh cabin mate, explained that the narrow tracks are better for the high-speed passenger trains of China and the wider ones of central Asia for hauling heavy loads.

Her son was returning from studying Chinese in Xian. "English is the most important language in the world," he told us, "and Chinese is the second." He is hoping to win a spot to study international relations in a good Chinese university.

And thus we left China and its national "bird," the construction crane that never stops building bigger and higher "nests" across its sprawling cities. We left China, but not its influence.

Later, on the road from northern Tajikistan south across the eleven-thousand-foot-high Anzob Pass to the capital city of Dushanbe, our car swung past a convoy of blue-tarped Chinese trucks. A Chinese company had contracted to build the new highway. In downtown

29

A central Asian street sign shows the distance to Dushanbe (Tajikistan), Tokyo, Chicago, and Paris.

Tashkent, Uzbekistan, an elegant Chinese restaurant tempted central Asian customers to branch beyond their ubiquitous shish kebab and osh (rice cooked with mutton, carrots, and onions.)

"These central Asian apricots have the highest natural sugar content in the world," an expatriate businessman explained as we sat in his apartment, sipping green tea with lemon and nibbling on dried apricots and candy-coated almonds.

For more than a year he'd been partnering with a local businessman to export dried apricots from central Asia to North America, where the luscious, deep-orange fruit are packaged and sold under a registered trademark. Working closely with local apricot farmers, the businessman is helping to improve productivity by fighting pests like the apricot bore and teaching new ways of pruning. He's also helping to bring local drying and packaging techniques up to western standards. As we walked though the orchards, he stroked the dark brown trunks of apricot trees like old friends.

Yet his first love is not apricots. He's also walking with local believers who meet in Turkic house churches—not giving financial assistance, but sharing encouragement, counsel, literature, and connections to the broader network of other followers of Jesus.

So we sat on the floor with him and his family in the home of a local family heading up a network of house churches. Darkness fell as we ate osh together. Electricity is rationed in the villages, and finally at six o'clock, when we could no longer see each other's expressions, the lights came on, only to go off again suddenly at seven thirty.

As we sang, prayed, and ate together, the local believers brimmed with stories of God's work in their lives. Government representatives had recently interrogated most members of the house churches. None were cowed; all confessed their faith and appealed to their freedom of worship according to their nation's laws. God had provided what they needed for their home, even down to the exact amount they'd needed for a certain light fixture.

A shoveler in northern Afghanistan keeps the road free of drifting sand.

Then a visitor from Russia shared his testimony. He'd gone there to work, but had grown lukewarm in faith. Last night he'd had a dream in which he'd been instructed to come to this house and get right with God. In his dream he'd also seen foreign strangers. He came, and here were people from the United States whom he'd never met. On the way home, the businessman confided, "Things are happening so fast I don't even have time to write them down. We really feel like we're joining God in what he is already doing here."

But the businessman would never have gotten to the region and connected with this emerging movement if not for his work with the apricot farmers. Eventually he hopes the business will create jobs for thirty or forty people. They are developing a facility for drying, sorting, and packaging large quantities of locally grown apricots. They also have secured a grant from a European firm to transform an old warehouse into a packing facility.

Another man and woman teach business English in a local university and in an orphanage. Their friendships with students and university colleagues open windows into a world they'd never have entered back home.

An engineer and nurse work among the rural poor, issuing microcredit loans, helping to develop village roads and water systems and to improve healthcare. A woman does business consulting and leads team-building seminars for Chinese companies in a large coastal city. All these are there, living, serving, and witnessing out of love for Christ and for the people among whom they live, not simply for a business that turns a buck.

Some criticize the "sneaky" way these Christian witnesses gained residence in their foreign homes. Their work is not done in the name of any mission organization, although most of them have sending groups back home. Are they deceptive?

We sometimes speak of "creative access" or "tentmaking" as

Gypsy children playing marbles.

though they were modern terms for a new phenomenon necessitated by the changing focus on the least-reached regions of the world, those that do not grant missionary visas to foreign Christians.

Yet there is little new about creative access. True, many Christian witnesses of the past hundred years became accustomed to the pattern of formally entering a country, registering as a mission, and dividing the country among missions in "comity" arrangements. All of this was based on the protection granted them by western colonial governments. But is Christian mission most ideally a function of colonialism?

When Mennonite missionaries first entered Tanzania in 1934, they were sent to the Lake Region on the shores of Lake Victoria, where no other mission was working. It was considered a less desirable region because of the plethora of small tribal groups. They could freely work as missionaries under the protection of the British Empire to establish schools and hospitals, which they did. God blessed that witness.

But there had been no such freedom when Jesuit missionary Matteo Ricci entered China in 1583. He developed two main principles for the mission: (1) make no secret of faith, but do not emphasize the missionary purpose, and (2) try to win the attention of the Chinese by demonstrating a knowledge of things in which they show great interest, like western science and learning.

Following these principles, Ricci taught mathematics and astronomy and prepared a map of the world that astonished educated Chinese with the possibility that China might not be the center of the world. He was also a master linguist, memorizing extensive sections of the Chinese classics and learning to write hundreds of Chinese characters. He dressed in the Confucian scholars' garb and mandated this for the rest of the Jesuit team.

With this appeal to the interests and needs of the Chinese, he and the Jesuit mission, which was barely tolerated, gradually won their way into the confidence and respect of Chinese leaders.[15] Yet none of

Central Asian women study English and medicine.

this was dependent on colonial occupation by a western power. It was sixteenth-century creative access, not unlike the contemporary agriculturalists, teachers, medical workers, businesspeople, and engineers who go with their skills to many nations with a vision for sharing Jesus—with no missionary visas from governments to support them.

When William Carey's team first arrived in Calcutta in 1793, they were not welcomed by the British East India Company. The emerging British Empire did not encourage missionaries. To survive and gain residence, Carey found employment on an indigo plantation. This was eighteenth-century creative access. Not until 1800 were they able to establish a mission base in the colony of another western nation, Denmark, at neighboring Serampore.

Later, when Carey's fame as a translator and scholar earned him a job at the government college, he supported much of the mission work with his earnings—keeping only fifty pounds of his 1,800-pound salary for himself. He was a "tentmaker" all his life, starting with shoes in England.

Today Christians teach English in the very heart of the Muslim world or work as maids in the homes of wealthy Middle Easterners. All the while, Jesus shines through. African, Indonesian, and Filipino Christians who live and work in the Middle East are becoming more intentional about their calling as missionaries. The Spirit of God does not need a missionary visa or a residence permit as a religious worker.

The upshot, we think, is that it is not deceptive to be who we are. Deception creeps only in when we claim to be who we are not. All Christian missions entail the risk of rejection by those to whom we go, and all authentic cross-cultural missions include some form of creative access.

Chapter 3

Missionary Societies

We were sitting with a central Asian missionary team, a fascinating blend of nations and cultures just right for a Silk Road city. It was half western and half eastern. The easterners were all from South Korea, the new dynamo in long-term evangelical missions at the beginning of the twenty-first century. The others were from Switzerland, Canada, the United States, England, and Scotland. An absent member of the group was from Indonesia.

All belonged to the same missionary society. All met weekly for worship, prayer, teaching, and table fellowship. All used the same trade language—English. All were evangelical but international, interdenominational, and long-term. Together they are committed to the spiritual frontiers of our time, going to peoples and places where the church is weak or nonexistent.

With some in the group, we were old friends. With others, this week's acquaintances were already becoming delightful new partners in mission. Richard shared a meditation from Scripture, then the group plunged into a morning of practical teaching on conflict resolution, complete with role playing of confession and forgiveness.

Missionary societies along the Silk Road have undergone profound changes through the centuries, yet they are easily recognizable as close kin in every era. This one was not unlike that of Hudson Taylor in the nineteenth century (China Inland Mission); the Jesuit pioneers (Francis Xavier, Matteo Ricci) in the sixteenth century to India, Japan, and China; or the Persian mission to the White Huns of central Asia in the sixth century.

All these societies called for lives of intimate union with Christ, lifelong commitment to reaching those who had not yet heard the good news, radical faith, simple lifestyles, and readiness to join international teams. The common language might be Persian, Latin, or English, but in every case it was a highly usable trade language. In every era they were also committed to learning the heart languages of the people to whom they went.

Obedience might have been to a Persian or Armenian patriarch, a Roman pope, an English evangelical visionary, or a North

The foundations of a church in the ancient Turkish city of Sujab, near Bishkek, Kyrgyzstan.

American regional administrator, but in every era there was clear focus and a ready willingness to submit to authority. That submission was coupled with so much feisty focus on the task at hand and love for the people to whom they went that they were quite capable of challenging and changing past traditions of their homelands for the sake of Jesus.

An ancient Turkish tomb stone in central Asia. Could the man be holding a communion chalice?

Take Francis Xavier, for example. At the height of the European renewal movement of the sixteenth century that some call the Protestant Reformation,[16] he led the way in breaking European Christianity out of the stranglehold of a Christendom that was isolated from most of the rest of the world and even from many of its non-Roman Christians. It was a commitment to Jesus that led to radical steps in mission. Xavier could hardly have known what his steps of obedience initiated. But he took them, and world history was transformed.

When Xavier first reached India in 1542, he refused the fine lodging that had been prepared for him and chose instead to live in a poor little cottage. For ten years he served among the lowest of the low—lepers, slaves, sinners, the poorest of the poor—with Christlike compassion. Long before Mother Teresa of the twentieth century, Xavier had shared that same compassionate, incarnational love of Jesus.

He lived first in Goa, then a few years later, down on Cape Comorin among the pearl fishers. There "his mission was to the very young, the poor, and the illiterate."[17]

Go backward in time many centuries to the first Syrian homeless wanderers for Jesus who headed east with the good news, following the apostle Thomas as others in the West followed the apostle Paul. They had names like Addai, Aggai, and Mari.

Addai went as far as Edessa, Nisibis, Arabia, and the borders of Mesopotamia. He planted churches and regional centers of mission that later trained and sent bands of Christian witnesses east for many centuries. The great school of Edessa, which was forced to move farther east to Nisibis before the end of the fifth century, was the most outstanding of these centers. More than a Bible institute or theological seminary, it was a close-knit Christian community. Students were expected not only to leave the world and remain single as long as they were in school, but they also gave all their possessions into the common purse, rooming in small cell groups of two or three.

There was strict discipline, with prohibitions on theft, falsehood, immorality, witchcraft, and heresy. They were forbidden to go westward into Roman Byzantine territory, possibly to prevent political and social fraternization with the enemies of Persia, which would create greater persecution for Persian Christians.

And they were imbued with missionary vision, laying the foundations for the astonishing extension of the Church of the East across central Asia and into China. At the peak of enrollment in Nisibis, more than one thousand students overflowed the old camel caravanserai, then moved into dozens of small student dormitories provided by the gift of a Christian physician who served the Persian emperor.[18] No Prairie Bible Institute of the twentieth century was more filled with missionary vision and action than the schools of Edessa and Nisibis in those early centuries.

Aggai continued Addai's work. He went all around Babylon, up to the Armenians west of the Caspian Sea, and perhaps as far as the borders of India.

A woman making tea in an outdoor restaurant in Tajikistan.

Mari, another Syrian student of Addai, was also sent east from Edessa. But he became discouraged and begged the church to allow him to return home. The church told him to keep going. (They probably didn't have a human resources department.) So Mari plugged on in a series of difficult journeys that took him far to the east. Contrary to some popular ideas, most of the Syrian ascetics didn't sit on poles in the desert.[19]

Or take Hudson Taylor, the Yorkshire lad who many centuries later became the nineteenth-century apostle to China. In a history peopled with giants of the faith from William Carey on, Taylor towers in incredible achievement among the pioneers of the modern evangelical missionary movement.

A physical weakling, he was nevertheless the founder of the China Inland Mission, which at his death in 1905 had 825 members scattered all over China, traveling to places no one else dared to go. "Always on the move," wrote a British official, "the missionaries of this society have traveled throughout the country, taking hardship and privation as the natural incidents of their profession, never attempting to force themselves anywhere, they have made friends everywhere."[20]

One of Taylor's co-workers wondered when he had time for personal devotions. He witnessed Taylor's grueling schedule from early in the morning till late at night. While sleeping in the same tent, the co-worker once awoke in the middle of the night to see Hudson quietly get out of bed, light a candle, and spend an hour with God. Then Taylor was back to bed till morning dawned.

In every age, missionary societies blossom anew, taking fresh form appropriate to the renewing work of the Holy Spirit in the new season. Along the Silk Road we saw them everywhere—stretching, changing, asking the most fundamental questions about their existence and forms, yet everywhere imbued with the pioneering, sharp-edged focus that links them with all the others who had gone before.

At a time in which Christianity has spread in some form to every nation-state, why shouldn't every missionary society be thoroughly international, reflecting the fact that the last words of Jesus were given to every church in the world? Why should there be any diminution of the radical faith that propelled Mari, John of Reshaina, Francis Xavier, and Hudson Taylor alike? And why shouldn't members of every society be constantly alert for opportunities to connect with members of others, especially in those local communities where we find ourselves, led by the Spirit, laboring side by side?

It is, we think, along the Silk Roads of the twenty-first century where there exists the greatest opportunity for synergy among brothers and sisters of many societies. It is, in fact, already happening.

Chapter 4

_____

Bridging the Barriers

"Afghanistan is a country you have to dress up to enter," our friend said. She'd arrived by plane and said that as soon as the plane landed in Kabul, scarves appeared, as if by magic, on the heads of all female passengers.

We entered the country on foot, walking over the Friendship Bridge across the Amu Darya River that separates Afghanistan from Uzbekistan in the north. Suddenly Jewel's calf-length trench coat was painfully short, her colorful head scarf too small. We had stepped into another world. Our hosts outfitted Richard in light gray baggy pants with a matching long-sleeved, knee-length shirt. Jewel acquired two new scarves and a chador. "You'll blend in better," our hosts said. "You'll feel safer, and people will feel more comfortable around you."

Further north, as we reveled in the beauty of a central Asian capital on a picture-perfect autumn day, a young woman told us how her parents had met Jesus. "My father was a Turk, my mother a Russian," she said. "Until fourteen years ago they lived in St. Petersburg, where they had met and married. But things weren't going well for them, and they were on the verge of divorce. My father wanted to move back to his small, isolated town in central Asia; my mother didn't want to leave Russia.

"But then they met Jesus in St. Petersburg. My mother's attitude changed. She told my father she was willing to move back to central Asia with him. For the past fourteen years they've lived in that distant, isolated place, and my father is the pastor of its church—a house fellowship of believers.

"The authorities harass my father constantly, watching his every move. It's hard and costly to be a believer here, especially in the towns outside the capital."

We strolled among the stately, mature plane trees, arched in autumn gold above sun-speckled passages in parks between impressive government buildings, pausing to photograph the great central equestrian statue of Amur Temur (Tamerlane), then going on to the holy spot where the young woman and her husband had pledged their lives in marriage only two months earlier.

What a perfect example her parents are of the bridges of God, we thought. A Turk marries a Russian in a great western city far to the northwest. Jesus draws them to himself and then plants them squarely in the middle of one of the most unreached places on earth. They're bearing steady, faithful witness in a place where no western (or eastern) cross-cultural witness is likely to go anytime soon.

On the same day, we met a young taxi driver who was a very attractive witness to Jesus. "I love this city and my people," he said. "Isn't it beautiful? God created all this loveliness. And he wants all of us to know Jesus. I love to walk and pray. I pray not only for my country but for the whole world. Please pray for us; we pray for you.

"My parents outside the city are now also believers. At first they berated themselves for teaching me to speak Russian rather than Turkish. 'You have left our God to serve a foreign god, the Russian,' they said. But God led me to learn Turkish for the sake of my people. And when my parents saw the change in my life, they too came to Jesus."

We heard such stories repeatedly along the Silk Road. Sometimes we were tempted to ask, Should long-term, western, cross-cultural witnesses continue? The most effective witnesses are clearly those who don't represent human power and wealth but those who go with the power of the Holy Spirit—already carrying a divinely orchestrated blend of cultural and spiritual connectedness.

The authors in Afghani attire.

Yet everywhere we heard the sincere, urgent invitation, "Come walk with us." God is still preparing Christian "bridgers" of every variety, and many of them are in the West as well as the East. A bridger is a person who incorporates multiple cultures into their personal dynamic. Some stay a short time, others for life. The easterners are mostly from Korea, the westerners from many nations.

Because there are communities of Korean immigrants in central Asia, Korean witnesses in some places can initiate Korean-speaking congregations. Others use Russian, and still others learn the local Turkic or Persian languages.

One of the most well-known of these Koreans began a congregation seventeen years ago in central Asia. Today the congregation has a weekly attendance of more than five thousand and continues to attract many local Turkic people as well as members of other nationalities in the cosmopolitan capital city.

"We regularly evaluate what it is that attracts people to Jesus," the pastor said. "We invite people to rate our worship, sermons, and other aspects of our public services.

"I think I'm a pretty good preacher, but the Sunday morning sermons never get rated very high. We have great worship teams that lead the congregation in inspiring worship. The worship is rated higher than the sermons, but even that is not what most attracts people to Jesus."

What else could it be? we wondered. Then came the revelation.

"The part of our public worship service that always gets the highest marks is the time when our members tell how they met Jesus," he said.

"Every Sunday we ask three people from our congregation to share a brief testimony, and we give them a simple outline to follow. 'Tell us what your life was like before you met Jesus, how you met Jesus, and how your life is different now,' we say to them.

Shared taxis are a common form of transportation in central Asia.

"They do, and those stories are so moving and influential that many others come to Jesus as a result. Of course, we don't testify only. All of us, two by two, regularly pray for specific people who don't know Jesus yet. This is not to prepare us psychologically to talk with them or to do something for them. It is simply because we know God answers prayer.

"Of course, as we pray, the Holy Spirit sometimes nudges us to reach out to them in some way. But often we observe that there's nothing we do to persuade them to become followers of Jesus. The Holy Spirit just draws them in!"

We rejoiced at the simple, obedient faith of this young Korean who had come to central Asia seventeen years earlier with little experience and no track record as a pastor. Now he leads what is probably the largest Christian congregation in all of central Asia.

The western missionaries are typically more low-key. They're less likely to start traditional Christian congregations. They move alongside their neighbors and invite them to become Christians. When the neighbors accept, the missionaries meet with them in house churches and look for ways to multiply networks of house churches. Some of those networks are blossoming.

But often the work is discouraging. One witness told us that he'd been working for ten years, but there seemed to be little to show for it. He and his group are taking stock, asking what they should do differently.

The differences in "success" cannot be traced to nationality. North Americans, Koreans, and Europeans all have big challenges as spiritual bridgers. Generally, North Americans are too controlled by their wealth and are prone to try to control others. Koreans are not sensitive to the cultural differences between themselves and those to whom they go. Europeans are slow to take initiative and are sometimes perceived as emotionally cold.

An Afghan elder.

Of course, all such stereotypes break down, and there are many exceptions in each group. Yet we are all inveterate categorizers, and all too often the boxes fit.

What never stopped amazing us was that God was leading so many witnesses from different parts of the world to these distant, hard-to-reach mountains, deserts, and river valleys, and blending them together in reaching out to others in the name of Jesus. We saw the fruit of their commitment everywhere, in individuals, house churches, and publicly worshipping congregations.

The Sunday morning sermon we heard in a Turkic congregation in central Asia was particularly inspiring. The language was local, the pastor was Turkic, and the whole meeting was energizing, even in translation.

There were about sixty-five people in the room. The pastor was slight of build and short, with a pleasant smile. Nothing prepossessing here, we thought. He began his sermon with "Why do we meet here on Sunday?

"It is to hear God speak. We come because of what Jesus told us, 'Go and make disciples of every people group, baptizing them in the name of the Father, the Son, and the Holy Spirit, teaching them to obey everything I command you.'

"Remember Gamaliel's words in Acts. 'If this is from God, you can't stop it!' And it has never stopped. Yes, Jesus was killed and his disciples scattered. But this movement we're part of is from God! Jesus rose from the dead.

"Some people think we come to church to get money. How many of you get money here?"

There were no hands.

"No! We come because Jesus is real. He changed our lives. We come because we *want* to. What is a disciple anyway? Yes, a disciple is a learner, a student. But we are not just people with our heads full of knowledge. A disciple is one who does the things the teacher

Ferrying across the Caspian Sea from Aktau, Kazakhstan to Baku, Azerbaijan.

does. An auto mechanic is not just someone who knows how to fix cars. He fixes them. Our job is to make disciples. Some people share the good news every day, others hardly ever share. We say 'come,' but Jesus says 'go.' Going is action.

"There are all kinds of Turkic people. We already have friends and relatives aplenty. Let's go to them. Our main thing is Jesus' Great Commission. I should be a disciple maker, sharing what I know. I don't have to be perfect. Jesus is Lord, not Russia or my country.

"Let's ask, 'God, whose heart are you working in? Whose heart are you preparing for Jesus?' If we ask God, he will show us. It's so simple. Let's pray for God to lead us to prepared people, then go to them and build a positive relationship. God will show us what to do with them."

The congregation and the pastor were in constant interaction as he spoke. Laughter, questions asked and answered, and shouts of "yes" rolled back and forth. No one was sleeping.

"Go with the assurance that you're right with God. Go with faith. Share the Word. Teach your friends how to read the Word, how to pray, and *stay in touch with them.* Model the life of Christ.

"There are more believers in Africa and Latin America now than in Europe and North America. Now Asia is joining Africa and Latin America!"

He ended his talk by displaying a brochure he had found about prayer triplets. Then he challenged the congregation to form these triplets to pray for those around them who are not yet believers.

Hearing his sermon and sitting in that thriving congregation, we realized that in this great, landlocked, remote, and mountainous region there is nevertheless plenty of world awareness. Furthermore, the good news is being proclaimed and lived with attractive and passionate joy.

The bridges (and the bridgers) of God are in place.

Chapter 5

House Churches and Church Houses

Walking the wide, tree-lined streets of his city, our friend described his parents' situation. "There is no church building in their town. There's not even a house church. So it's hard for them. But they are quiet believers in Jesus in their own home. They enjoy visiting the church here when they come to the city. We have a big worship team. I play guitar and help to lead worship.

"Today there are about five thousand Turkic believers in our nation. Most of us worship in house churches since we are not allowed to register for worship in public places. Just last week, in another place, some of the believers were having a birthday party. It was raided by the police, and my brother is still in prison."

∞

From its earliest beginnings, the Christian church has often met in houses. The New Testament, of course, makes reference to churches in homes.[21] But in the centuries since, Christians have more frequently met in larger gatherings in public places.

The first known Christian church building was in the town of Dura-Europos, on the west bank of the Euphrates River on the Roman-Persian border. Sometime in the early third century, a group of Christians created a meeting place in a private home, keeping the front rooms plain and undecorated so as not to attract attention. It was a house-turned-church that retained the appearance of a house. For many centuries it lay buried under a collapsed city wall until it was discovered in the twentieth century. In it were a baptistery and paintings on the wall, depicting Christ carrying the lost sheep and the three Marys coming to the tomb.[22]

Before that time, most Christians living in the Roman and Persian empires apparently met in homes. To do otherwise could have invited unfriendly attention. Especially in the Roman Empire, persecution of Christians often flared. But quite apart from the danger of persecution, the very nature of the church invited intimate household fellowship among brothers and sisters in Christ.

Back in the United States, we debate the merits of megachurches and microchurches. The "cell church" model includes both, we say, with large public gatherings for celebration alternated with small-group meetings in homes for intimate fellowship and accountability.

But in many parts of the world, there is little choice. Large gatherings are not an option because governments don't permit them or allow Christian meetinghouses to be built. In the early 1980s, when our family first moved to a community along the western end of the Silk Road, not far from the Euphrates River, there were no Christian believers in our city. As people met Jesus and we began to meet for fellowship, we met in homes. That was the only option.

Soon one of the new believers offered his home as a regular meeting place. He removed a wall between two rooms, and that

The tomb of Ali the Prophet in Mazar-e-sharif, Afghanistan.

became our "church house." Though we had no baptistery or paintings on the walls, it was a Christian meeting place not unlike that in Dura-Europos eighteen centuries before.

Traveling the Silk Road, we looked for the remains of church buildings dating from the earliest east-to-east spread of Christianity following the first apostles. The remains are no longer obvious, but they are being found in many places by archaeologists.

The first we visited was near Xian, where we traveled into the countryside to see the only known building remaining from the earliest Syrian mission to China. At a village nearby, we mounted horses and rode to a leaning pagoda built by Christians in the T'ang Dynasty, seven hundred years after Christ. Beside the pagoda stood a replica of the famous Nestorian Tablet, which is kept in a museum in Xian. In a couple of small rooms nearby were a few reproductions of paintings found in the pagoda and other evidence of early Christian presence in China.

Tourists stream from every part of the world to Xian to visit the famous terracotta warriors found in the tombs of the Chinese emperor who united all of China two hundred years before Christ. We did, too, and they were an awesome sight—line after line of life-sized models of Chinese soldiers, each apparently modeled after a particular individual in the army of Qin Shihuang (259-210 BC).

The Zenkov Cathedral in Almaty, Kazakhstan, the largest wooden cathedral in the world.

But for us, seeing the remains of that other kingdom was the supreme joy of discovery at the eastern end of the Silk Road. When our ancestors in Europe were still pagan barbarians, the good news had already been taken by Syrian Christians all the way to the heart of China. That visit to the ancient pagoda was as close as we came to religious pilgrimage.

Later, far to the west in the Chuy Valley of northern Kyrgyzstan, east of Bishkek, we visited an ancient Silk Road city (Sujab) near the village of Aq-beshim. There at the southeastern corner of the crumbling city walls of this Karakhanid Turkish city lie the foundations of a Christian church. At another ancient site nearby called Burana, we saw the crosses of those early central Asian Christians, scant remains of Christian communities that flourished among the Turks during the Dark Ages of the West.

Where, we wondered, did most of our brothers and sisters in central Asia worship in those years? Were their meetings mostly in the great Silk Road metropolitan centers of Herat, Balkh, Merv,

Samarkand, and Kashgar? Bishops and archbishops lived in those cities, we knew. Those were the settled Persians and Turks.

There were few remains to explore—just the endless, empty steppes. How many "yurt churches" meeting in the tent-like dwellings still used today were there in those centuries? How many village homes and chapels of mud or wood in the "land between the rivers"?

Today, there are both house churches and church houses in central Asia. The Russian Orthodox legacy remains in the great cities. In Almaty, Kazakhstan, we were enthralled by the ethereal worship chants in the magnificent Zenkov Cathedral, reputed to be the largest wooden cathedral in the world. In Tajikistan, we attended a Baptist church founded by Russians but continued now under central Asian leadership.

For the central Asian believers themselves, the choices are simple, but not easy. Some countries are more open than others, but there is a certain tentativeness almost everywhere. Shall we worship in public in Russian or in private in Kazakh, Kyrgyz, Tajik, or Uzbek? There are

A traditional church in Armenia.

few reports of new public churches being registered; more frequently, old ones are being closed.

∽

Just before setting out along the Silk Road, we traveled one September day to the beautiful Emmental of Switzerland from where our European Anabaptist ancestors had fled the pressures of the state church. There we stopped at Langnau and visited the world's oldest Anabaptist congregation in continuous existence, founded in 1530.

The Mennonite church house at Langnau looks more like a house than a church, and for good reasons. For centuries the Anabaptists of the Emmental had been hounded from their homes for heresy and often sent away to Bern via the local castle at Trachselwald, where they were imprisoned, deported, executed, or sentenced to service as galley slaves. The Anabaptist house-church tradition, still preserved by Amish Mennonite communities in the United States, began in those days.

Shades of Dura-Europos on the west bank of the Euphrates in the early third century. Shades of central Asia. Shades of our house church on the western end of the Silk Road in the twentieth century. Shades of the Meserete Kristos Church of Ethiopia.[23] Shades of dozens of other places around the world where brothers and sisters meet quietly in homes, especially when public attention would be unfriendly.

It's not easy to maintain the tradition of house churches when a society gives freedom to meet in larger public gatherings for worship. Then we gather publicly, joyfully, inviting others to join us. The house church is usually seen as an addendum, an extra—and often not fully church. We begin to assume that church is present where buildings are built to house the flourishing congregations. But we know better.

We wonder whether the most essential and definitive form of the Christian meeting place is the house church. If so, anything else, like our spacious buildings and magnificent cathedrals with their attendant organizational structures, is the addendum, the extra. It certainly seems so along the Silk Road.

Chapter 6

'Underground' Christians

One of our foreign friends had recently been expelled from his country along with workers from dozens of other nongovernmental organizations. Another still lived there, grateful to have found a job that permits ongoing residence. "The Turkic-speaking churches all lost their registration," he said. "So we meet in small home groups. Right now we're not even singing. Sometimes we'll quote the words of a hymn together in a corporate act of worship. The government is trying to decide what to do with us."

When our family lived in the western Turkic world during the 1980s, we discovered a surprising ignorance coupled with genuine curiosity about Christian faith. Most of the people in our city had never met a Christian or seen a Bible.

As we taught English in the university and opened our home to friends, students, and neighbors, a small house church emerged. We knew that a hundred years earlier our region had been dotted with hundreds of Christian churches and schools. Some churches had been sizeable—one thousand members and more. Now the buildings were used as concert halls, museums, prisons, barns.

Breakfast on the road in Tajikistan.

There had been nothing secret about the thriving Christian communities that lived as a *millet*, a religious minority community within the Ottoman Empire with a legal and recognizable identity. The tragedies of World War I and the breakup of the empire led to death for many, coupled with massive exchanges of population.

After the empire's end in the 1980s, the constitution upheld religious freedom, but to become a Christian was hardly acceptable. Our little house church grew slowly. There were members of an extended family, a university student, and a young businessman.

Then came our deportation, followed two years later by arrests and interrogation. House-church leaders were imprisoned for a time. As one of the brothers suffered in prison, he cried out to God, "Why do I have to suffer like this?"

God spoke clearly to his spirit, "You are suffering so that other of your countrymen will know that some of you are followers of Jesus." And indeed this was happening as the story of his arrest as a "traitor" was plastered on the front pages of the country's major newspapers.

The vulnerable little house fellowship scattered, but all across the country were people who longed for information about the gift of God's grace in Jesus. Many found a new window opened into their homogeneous world.

Today, all along the Silk Road, hundreds of unpublicized house churches study the Bible, pray, encourage one another, and worship—sometimes openly in song and sometimes mouthing hymns in unison. Just as the apostle Paul spoke of himself centuries ago, they are "known yet unknown."

In an eastern city, we met a young couple who are popular English university professors. But they also help to run an unpublicized training center for young people committed to carrying the gospel westward "back to Jerusalem" no matter what the cost. They are beginning to go. We wept as we saw their zeal and their passion, when we heard the stories of their suffering.

One fourteen-year-old girl began to evangelize in the streets of her city against the violent opposition of her father, a leading political party official. "You must believe in Jesus, or you will go to hell," was the simple, forthright message she and other young people tramped the streets to share. God proved his word with signs and wonders. Her father, whose life was miraculously spared when he fell down a well, became a believer along with hundreds of others in their village.

In the book *Back to Jerusalem*, three Chinese house-church leaders described their strategy for missions as they left their country and traveled westward toward Europe:

> Termites are very hard to detect. They do their destructive work inside the walls of homes and underneath floorboards.

> Usually the owner of the house has no clue that his magnifi-
> cent structure is being eaten away until it is too late, and it col-
> lapses in a heap. The termite can do what even an elephant is
> unable to do. . . . By God's grace, [as missionaries] we will be
> like little worms, ants, and termites, quietly but consistently
> working away, loosening the foundations of [false religious
> understandings].[24]

There have always been such hidden Christians, some hidden
away in an upper room "for fear of the Jews." Others scrawling the
sign of the fish on the walls of the Roman catacombs, quietly yet
boldly testifying to an alien identity at odds with the ruling powers.
Some grow cold and no longer witness; others share courageously,
but without the privilege of public recognition.

The story of early Roman Catholic Christianity in Japan is
that of Christians who, after intense opposition by the ruling powers, maintained a secluded faith for two hundred and fifty years.
Roman Catholic missionary Francis Xavier led the first Christian
mission to Japan in 1549. The Christian faith was attractive to all
classes of society, including the ruling shogunate. The church grew
rapidly, to as many as three hundred thousand by 1614, when the
leadership of the recently unified Japan turned violently anti-
Christian. It ordered all churches closed, deported the western missionaries, and prohibited all practice of Christianity.

During the next thirty years, the entire Christian population
was systematically burned, strangled, starved, tortured, or driven
underground. There were 4,045 well-documented martyrdoms by
1651, and executions continued until 1697, when the government
was satisfied that it had eradicated the church.

Japan feared Christianity as a threat to the unity of the nation.
It suspected that Christian missionaries were the spearhead of western imperialism intruding from without.[25] Unfortunately, their sus-

Merchants selling nan, the bread of central Asia.

picions were not entirely unwarranted, despite the good intentions of the missionaries.

It was two hundred and fifty years before Roman Catholic missionaries could return. To their astonishment, in 1865 they discovered thirty thousand hidden Christians who had survived the long years of silence and supposed eradication. They had made certain accommodations to Buddhism for registration and funerals, but they had maintained secret Christian worship and symbols.[26] Today half of all Catholics in Japan are descendants of these hidden Christians.

When harassment of the small evangelical church in the western Turkic world turned public in 1988, we asked a local believer how he felt about the negative publicity in the media. "When I was a secret believer," he said, "I looked for some way to connect with other believers. All across our country there are thousands of unknown believers. When they see this publicity, they'll be encouraged to learn that there are many others who believe in Jesus like they do. They won't feel so alone."

We had the privilege of discipling a man in his thirties who had decided as a child he wanted to be a Christian. When we first met him, he pulled out a copper cross he'd worn on a leather thong around his neck, hidden under his clothes. "I felt like a tiny, green shoot trying to break out of the desert floor," he said. "Now there's water. I can grow." He opened his home to begin a small house church in his neighborhood.

Once people meet Jesus and hear of the love of God and the good news of his heavenly kingdom, there is a sweetness that lingers, a hope that beckons. A hidden believer in south-central Asia said she'd first heard of Jesus when her only sister died. In their grief, her grandmother whispered, "If Jesus had been here, she would not have died. Jesus has the power to open blind eyes and make lame people walk."

This piqued her interest in Jesus and, sometime later, while studying in a neighboring country, she read a Bible for the first time. Later Christian aid workers filled in some missing links in her understanding, and she began to consider herself a follower of Jesus.

As an educated woman living under a strict Islamic regime, she risked her life to work and translate for foreign aid workers, sliding through checkpoints in her dark blue burka.

Like so many of her fellow citizens, this woman has seen incredible tragedy. Her father and other family members were murdered for political reasons while she was in university, and a rocket attack during the mujahidin years killed her son and brother. Another son is bedridden with an incurable illness. Her husband died of a heart attack. But she clings to Jesus, quietly giving her grandchildren Christian names.

She can't discuss these kinds of things openly. It is illegal to become a Christian in her country, where the penalty for conversion from Islam is death. But she is quite sure she has a sister and brother-in-law who are also believers. She's seen them reading the Bible and praying. They don't keep Ramadan or go to the mosque. Their lives are pure and radiant. Her mother also believes.

"A religion may spread through violence," she said, "but true Christianity spreads through preaching, love, and good deeds."

As we crossed central Asia, we wondered how many other unknown Christians prayed alone in hope. Why are governments so afraid of the followers of Jesus? And we remembered the thousands suffering persecution in Asia and the whole communities that have been snuffed out.

As we sipped tea with cardamom and flipped through stacks of elegant handmade carpets in a well-known Silk Road city, suddenly we saw the old Turkmen pattern we'd been looking for—Golgotha woven into the rug. There it was, in rich patches of maroon and tan camel and sheep wool, the unmistakable motif of a hill with three crosses.

"What do you call this pattern?" we asked.

The salesman shrugged. "It's a traditional Turkmen pattern famous here. No other name."

Did the village women and girls who hand-knotted the rugs know they were weaving the faith of their Christian ancestors into them? The striking design flew in the face of the assumption that "to be Turkic is to be Muslim."

A vibrant group of Kazakh Christians treated us to a sumptuous meal in their yurt. As they presented the head of a sheep slaughtered to prepare the famous national dish *beshparmak* (literally, "five fin-

A hanging on the wall of a restaurant in Bukhara, Uzbekistan. Might it be a depiction of the Last Supper?

gers," which are used to eat from a common platter), they remarked that according to their tradition they always scored the head of the sheep with the sign of the cross before presenting it to the guest of honor.

"Before we were Christians, we never knew why we did this. It was just an old custom. But now that we've heard of Jesus, we know that our ancestors must have been Christians. These old roots are bearing fruit."

Many of the ancient church buildings in central Asia were destroyed by Genghis Khan and Tamerlane. There were frequent waves of hostility, persecution, isolation, discrimination. The Soviet era also was not kind to the church. Yet faithful communities persisted—sometimes open, sometimes "underground."

There are tantalizing signs of faith. One evening as we sat in a basement restaurant in Bukhara, Uzbekistan, we noticed a design in a wall hanging that looked like saints with halos. Perhaps we'd just visited too many Russian Orthodox cathedrals. Then we noticed that the "saints" were arranged in a circle around something that looked like a chalice. Just for fun we counted them. There were twelve.

We could never prove it, but in our minds the colorful Uzbek wall hanging was of the twelve disciples of Jesus at the Last Supper, many of whom fanned out across central Asia, bearing witness to Jesus. It also became a symbol for us of the many hidden Christians worshipping alone or in small house churches. They're there in little groups of ten or twelve, almost unnoticed, but vibrant and beautiful.

Just as Jesus trusted the evangelization of the whole world to his little band of twelve, so these unremarkable house churches pop up in the most unexpected places, transforming their worlds with a far greater power than meets the eye.

Chapter 7

Foreign Witnesses and Local Leadership

"Since many of the foreign workers have been expelled from our country, we're having to take charge of things," the young pastor explained. Then he outlined excitedly the network of house churches that stretches across regional and denominational lines. His eyes shone with pride, determination, and ownership.

"Before I became a Christian, I didn't even speak my mother's tongue. I just spoke Russian and English. But that has all changed. God motivated me to learn our language so my people know Jesus is not the so-called 'Russian god' but the God of all peoples—including us!"

Earlier, while rattling across western China ("Chinese Turkestan," Xinjiang Uygur Autonomous Region) by train, a contemporary, cross-cultural witness in China described the rapid growth of the house-church movement in China: "The leaders of the house churches in our city asked us to assist them with evangelistic home Bible studies while we were studying Chinese," he said. "The combi-

Bukhara, Uzbekistan.

nation of foreign Christians and local leaders seemed to work well, and our Bible study prospered, with quite a few young people coming to Christ.

"A western mission agency with a strong focus on initiating church-planting movements also contacted the local house-church leaders and urged them to adopt their strategy for evangelism. The local leaders listened respectfully and appreciated their emphasis on evangelism but felt that their approach to church life was too one-sided, not holistic enough. The Chinese wanted to make use of all the gifts in building the church, not just that of evangelism.

"The Chinese leaders sensed that the westerners were more interested in promoting their strategy than in learning from the experience of the local house-church movement in its rapid multiplication. Yet they wanted to encourage the western missionaries. So they found ways to benefit from partnership in evangelism with the westerners. Without trying to explain their strategy, they quietly continued their own broader approach to church development."

We listened and rejoiced. Such a church will not easily be led astray by the sincere but sometimes misguided zeal of cross-cultural witnesses who may impose alien agendas that run counter to what the Holy Spirit is doing. The church in China is growing in maturity, combining appropriate encouragement of those who come from the West with Spirit-guided focus by Chinese leadership.

All along the Silk Road we reflected on the interplay of foreign witnesses and local leadership, a challenge to the church in every era. The cross-cultural witness is a "bridge" for the good news from a place where the church is strong to another where it is weak. The same witness may also become a vital partner and sensitive participant in the newer church. But the danger remains of substituting the Spirit-led direction of the local believers with the traditions of the sending church.

The earliest east-to-east missionaries to central Asia and China were Syrians and Persians of the Church of the East, usually traveling in bands, just as today's western missionaries do. Like the Roman Catholic and Eastern Orthodox missionaries

Cherry juice and history sustained us on a 60-hour train trip across Kazakhstan.

of the church of the West, they went with a strong commitment to the ecclesiastical authorities of the sending churches. For the Syrians and Persians, this ecclesiastical authority was usually the patriarch of the Church of the East (Nestorian) at Seleucia-Ctesiphon, Persia's capital city. But such geographically external authority has often thwarted the development of local leadership, in our time as well as in earlier centuries.

Furthermore, all of us instinctively prefer and constantly use our native languages. Yet sometimes we hold them too sacred. When the stone-carved Nestorian Tablet was erected near Xian, China, in 781, almost one hundred and fifty years after the arrival of Syrian missionaries to the imperial courts of the T'ang Empire in 635, the church of China was still overseen by Syrian rather than Chinese leaders.

Perhaps this was a reason for its vulnerability when the T'ang Dynasty finally ended in 907. Even with ecclesiastical deference to the Persian patriarch far away to the west, stronger indigenous Chinese leadership might have more skillfully led in adapting to the changing Chinese political situation at that time, and the church might have prospered.

But when the T'ang Dynasty fell, the Church of the East in China went into a period of eclipse, perhaps disappearing completely for several centuries during the Sung Dynasty, starting in 960.[27] Only with the coming of the Mongol Yuan Dynasty (Genghis Khan, Kublai Khan, and successors from 1162 to about 1370) do we again find numerous accounts of Christians in China.[28]

The challenges continue today. A few weeks before we arrived in Bishkek, a western worker completed a survey of mature Kyrgyz church leaders, inviting them to evaluate the cross-cultural witnesses who work among them. The results were sobering and thought provoking. The study identified three issues that have a huge impact on local perceptions of cross-cultural witnesses in Kyrgyzstan: lifestyles, murky methodologies, and their tendency to control.

Whereas Christian witnesses tend to categorize themselves on the basis of profession, nationality, and sending organization, the

Hospitable companions who shared our compartment across the steppes of Kazakhstan.

local Kyrgyz leaders generally use other categories. These are workers who are (1) good examples, (2) rich, (3) too busy, (4) unclear in what they are doing, or (5) bad examples. In their evaluations, both American and Korean witnesses tend to be overly controlling; Americans are often critiqued for the use of their wealth; Koreans are considered less sensitive culturally; and Europeans have a positive blend of generosity, personal engagement in evangelism, and lack of pride.[29]

The comments of mature Kyrgyz leaders regarding the cross-cultural witnesses among them make it abundantly clear that not only seventh-century Syrians in China but also twenty-first-century westerners and easterners in central Asia struggle with how best to raise up a new church in a foreign culture: how to nurture local leaders, how long to stay, how to give a winsome witness for

Jesus, how to make a living, how to relate to the ecclesiastical or missional authorities that sent them. These and similar questions have challenged apostles along the Silk Road in the centuries since Pentecost.

Chapter 8

When Does Adapting Become Unfaithful?

That's not a painting of God, is it? We peered up at the dome of St. Nicholas Russian Orthodox Cathedral in Almaty, Kazakhstan. There sat Jesus on the right side of a stern, white-bearded man. Accustomed to seeing depictions of the life of Jesus in Bible storybooks, we'd formed mental images of him. But God? This seemed almost blasphemous. No one has seen God's face and lived. He is inscrutable. Other. Jesus shows us the face of God. The creation shows his handiwork but cannot contain him. He is the Creator, the omnipotent One.

We remembered the folk song from our college years: "What color is God's skin? What color is God's skin? I say it's black, brown, yellow, it's red and it's white; every man's the same in the good Lord's sight." We left troubled.

In St. Nicholas Cathedral we walked among the paintings and icons that covered the walls, ceilings, and dome. We were awed by their beauty as we had been the day before by the sheer loveliness of the majestic Zenkov Cathedral across town. At both churches, the exits were crowned by a scene of the last judgment, with heaven on the left and hell on the right. We stood for a long time before a scene of red-haired Mary anointing Jesus' feet, reveling in the beauty that flowed from the age-old Russian expression of the Christian family.

Many centuries after Christianity came from the east with Persian and Syrian missionaries along the Silk Road, it had come again with Russian rulers from the northwest, clad in Eastern Orthodox dress. Whenever we talked with central Asians, they referred to the Christian God as a foreign, Russian god. And now it seemed that what had come with the Russians was departing with the Russian exodus from central Asia.

When the Soviet Union disbanded and became the Commonwealth of Independent States in 1991, the new nations of central Asia (Kazakhstan, Kyrgyzstan, Tajikistan, Uzbekistan, and Turkmenistan) naturally began to adopt new national languages.

A central Asian artist's depiction of the prodigal son.

They created administrations appropriate to the local people, which governed from places like Tashkent and Bishkek, rather than receiving direction from Moscow far to the northwest. The Russians who lived in central Asia began to move back home.

Simultaneously the Russian Orthodox congregations that were scattered across the Turkic/Mongol/Persian world are disappearing with their departure. Only in the great urban centers such as Almaty and Tashkent do the cathedral congregations still appear to be flourishing with the faithful. In Almaty, we were moved with the piety and worship of the congregation that gathered in Zenkov Cathedral.

With the Russians, the Baptists and Mennonites had also come. Some of these were Germans displaced to the east by Stalin's deportations. To the Russian and German churches, too, there was always a trickle of central Asians, some of whom met Jesus in life-changing ways. Frequently we saw evidence of how God was using that Russian imperial phase of colonization and rule to reintroduce Christian faith in communities where the memory of the first churches of central Asia had long since faded.

For example, we met a local pastor who, as a result of the witness of Russian-speaking German Baptists, had accepted Jesus in prison. He was leading in the dynamic revitalization of a Russian-speaking Baptist congregation, building bridges of outreach beyond the old ethnic boundaries.

We saw that God doesn't waste anything. Empires, fossilizing religious traditions, naïve or perceptive cross-cultural witnesses from many nations, inter-ethnic marriages—all are conscripted for kingdom use.

But what will endure? What is essential? What are the distinctions between that which is eternally significant and that which will be stripped away and burned like chaff?

Our joy in the beauty of St. Nicholas Cathedral was clouded by questions. Did we see the painting in the dome correctly? Was the man in the beard really an image of God the Father? Or was it perhaps St. Nicholas sitting beside Jesus? Santa Claus! But no, that couldn't be right. It must be a depiction of our Father God.

It is indeed God the Father, but does it not somehow do violence to his very nature to depict him sitting beside Jesus as a white-bearded man—like two men in a teahouse? What could this possibly mean to the people of central Asia, schooled as they now are in the worship of one God, Allah? Does it not fulfill all their stereotypes of the trinitarian Christian God as a debased form of tri-theism, or in this case, di-theism?

Is this a form of western Christian syncretism, shaped too richly by Hellenistic forms of theological contextualization, then transported across vast Russia eastward to central Asia? We were troubled and uncertain, determined to explore the meaning of the painting that perplexed and stimulated us.

As we traveled on, the issues of adaptation and faithfulness kept popping up.[30] We remembered the young lad at the site of the ancient church of Philadelphia in Alasehir, Turkey, who told us that the Christian trinity consisted of God the Father, God the Son, and God the Holy Virgin. The misunderstanding seemed to fit rather well the paintings in the traditional churches we visited, with the ever-present mother of Jesus.

But other questions came closer home to us as evangelical Anabaptist Christians. In one place we attended the dedication of a Christian church that had been built by a Korean businessman, not as the result of the presence of a Christian congregation but in hopeful anticipation of one. Perhaps as one result, local Christian leaders critiqued the cross-cultural missionaries among them partly on the basis of whether or not they built church buildings.[31] The "good examples" did not build churches; the "bad examples" did. Hmmm.

An Afghani man feeding pigeons outside a mosque.

In another country, we observed our brothers and sisters wrestling with the question of whether or not to register one expression of the Christian movement with the government. If they registered, they could worship openly and perhaps rent or buy centers for worship. If they did not, would they be doomed to exist only as house churches? But if they registered, would they be controlled?

This reminded us of China, home of the largest evangelical church in the world. There are two major expressions of Christianity there. One is the church legitimized by the government, the Three-Self Church. It is a national church that worships in public buildings and runs seminaries and printing presses. The other is the complex movement of house churches that is actually larger than the official church. The official church is more like a western state church, the house churches more like Anabaptists. Is one syncretistic, the other contextualized? If so, which is which?

Granddaughter Rachel and Ronald McDonald welcomed the authors back to the U.S. after the Silk Road pilgrimage.

The answers are neither obvious nor easy. Conclusions inevitably depend on starting points, and every generalization will be contested. But for us as grassroots western evangelicals with our particular missionary expressions, the "free church" nature of the house churches leads to greater affinity with them. Yet we are so accustomed to governmental legitimacy for our own churches that it is hard for us to imagine not having legitimacy as a goal, in China as well as in North America. So in that way we are drawn also to the "official" church.

We came, then, to the central questions. Adaptation to every local context—yes. Refusal to yield the core of the good news—yes. But at the end of the day, is it impossible to say yes to both?

We think not. There must be a way. Yet we are convinced that only the Holy Spirit can make it possible for us to walk that line in each new situation, saying yes with confidence. Furthermore, it's where we live in our native cultural home that walking it out is hardest and most important. Making decisions for others seems at times relatively easy, but making good decisions for ourselves—that's as hard as nails.

So the cross-cultural missionary always goes back home for the toughest questions.

Chapter 9

Christian Unity

"The Syrian evangelical church in a neighboring province didn't want to have fellowship with those of us from Muslim background," the western Turkic pastor said. "They were afraid it would limit their own ability to survive. You had to be from a Christian background to go to their church. But when the government closed their church, we went to the local government and protested. According to our constitution, there is freedom of religion. They should be allowed to worship freely. The government backed down. The Syrian pastor was profuse in his thanks to us. And now we fellowship together. We are all part of the body of Christ."

Our central Asian host spoke earnestly. "We are a network of house churches all over the country, divided into four regions. There are sixteen pastors, and we meet regularly for fellowship, prayer, and planning. We are sending evangelistic teams each year into different parts of our country, and soon we want to send international, cross-cultural teams. We represent about five hundred believers, but there are many others in different churches—Baptist, Pentecostal, and charismatic.

An ancient Syrian church in Diyarbakir, Turkey.

"Though there are different networks in our country, we fellowship and work together. We see ourselves as one body in Christ."

In another country a few days earlier, a Korean-American had told us how the foreign witnesses meet regularly for prayer and worship. Though they represent different sending organizations, they recognize and rejoice in their common focus, celebrating "one faith, one baptism, one Lord, one God and Father of all."

Twenty years earlier, while living in the western Turkic world, we had participated in fellowship and planning with all the foreign Christian witnesses from different parts of the world who lived in our nation. We met in each other's homes, prayed together, and worked together in countless ways. Then, we thought perhaps we were unique. But while traveling the Silk Road, we saw those same patterns repeated in many nations.

Somewhere near the border of Iran we happened into a weekly prayer gathering and discovered believers from Japan, Kazakhstan, and Bolivia engaged in fervent, joyous worship. All are serving as Christian witnesses in their city. They told us that there are also representatives of the Back to Jerusalem movement among them and reported with awe what God is doing in Iranian cities nearby.

We soon learned that there is no external sending organization that brings them all together. It is solely their faith in Jesus and their common purpose in reaching out in love to those around them. In just a few hours of fellowship, we felt ourselves part of their team, and we promised to stay in contact.

One of these newfound friends asked whether North Americans are still capable of long-term service or only short-term jaunts here and there. We reflected together. The answer for North Americans is surely both/and, but looking back at the United States through the eyes of a sister from a nation half a world away was sobering.

Have our habits of instant communication, food, travel, and

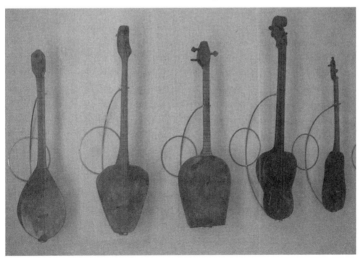

Stringed instruments originated in central Asia.

A Syrian archbishop in Mardin, Turkey.

access to information been translated into Christian missions as well? Are we capable of long-term, lifelong commitment? We hope so.

Reflecting on the sweep of Christian history along the Silk Road, it is evident that Spirit-given unity of life together in missions from many nations and cultures is not new. When John of Resh-aina and Thomas the Tanner dedicated themselves to Christian witness among the White Huns of Transoxiana (modern Uzbekistan, Tajikistan, and southwest Kazakhstan) five hundred years after Christ, they were soon joined by five others, one of whom was an Armenian bishop. Back home, the Armenian Monophysites and Persian Dyophysites debated the nature of Christ. Did Jesus have one, undifferentiated will, or was there a distinction between the human and divine in his nature?

Here, however, in the heart of central Asia, the seven men lived together on one jar of water and seven loaves of bread a day. They led an outstanding, holistic, and successful mission to the Mongol-Turkic peoples of their time. John, Thomas, and the Armenian bishop in particular persevered in dedicated witness and service.

From such service, which pushed aside and beyond the theological wrangles of Rome, Byzantium, Antioch, Alexandria, and Seleucia-Ctesiphon, the good news continued to stream eastward along the Silk Road. Who would have thought that Monophysites and Dyophysites would ever unite in mission?[32] Not their sending churches.

But then, who would have expected to find Japanese, Kazakh, and Bolivian believers united in worship and witness in central Asia in the twenty-first century? And who would have expected

Enjoying a plate of Uighur noodles in western China.

charismatics, Pentecostals, Baptists, and assorted others from the global body of Christ to pray and plan together in witness all across central Asia? Not their sending bodies or ecclesiastical centers.

Does mission, then, bring Christians together? Well, maybe.

But we think the answer lies deeper. Jesus brings people together, and where Jesus lives and reigns in intimate union with those he has called to himself, mission happens. Therefore, it does appear that mission brings believers together. In reality, though, it is Jesus.

There are, of course, many practical questions beyond these. What is God's pattern for ecclesiastical union? If indeed there is one body in Christ, should we not promote an organizational and organic union of all believers and churches in one great communion of believers worldwide? Many hope, pray, and labor for that end. If such an organization existed in obedience to our Lord, we would gladly join it. But we do not expect it in our lifetime.

In the meantime, we joyfully confess Jesus as Lord, acknowledging our union in Christ with all those who belong to him and looking for them everywhere. We especially look for those who are not yet believers, inviting them to become part of the one body that already exists as one in Christ.

We are convinced that our organic union in Christ is more important than any organizational expression of it.

Chapter 10

Empire and Church

One lovely fall day we sat in an outdoor café, enjoying lunch with new friends from an international church. Across the table sat a middle-aged French woman who had grown up in Mozambique. Her father had worked for a large, international, French-owned company. Now she was married to a businessman, and they'd lived all over the world. She shared the beautiful story of how she had come to faith in Christ during her years in China through the witness of international Christian friends.

"Before I became a Christian," she said, "my French identity was very important to me. You could say I was fiercely French! I'd never really lived in France, but I knew I was French. Now I don't care. My identity is in Christ."

In Samarkand, Uzbekistan, lies the quietly elegant Guri Amir Mausoleum, grave of Tamerlane (Amur Temur). It's now a place of pilgrimage for Uzbeks who gaze at maps of the expansive kingdom his ruthlessly effective military campaigns flung from China to Europe between 1387 and 1405. Uzbeks claim him in some oblique way as one of the founders of the modern state of Uzbekistan.

The kiosk at his grave sold pictures of him twinned with the modern Uzbek president, Islam Karimov. The implication is unmis-

takable: these are our heroes, our founders. Uzbekistan is free. Uzbekistan is rising. Tamerlane's statue has replaced Lenin's in the main square fronting the parliament buildings.

A local believer explained: "We're very tiny, and only in a few places do we still have the freedom to worship openly in churches. In most towns and villages we meet in homes, cell groups. We can't sing and worship freely. Maybe there are five thousand central Asian followers

Lenin still broods over Tajikistan.

of Jesus in our country. In the whole country there are maybe twenty thousand Christians. That includes Russians, local Koreans. It's okay for them to be Christian. But the government doesn't want us to use our mother tongue in our worship services. We have to use Russian.

"I know Amur Temur killed many people. But now our country is looking to him as a hero. My hero is Jesus. He loves everyone. I love to take prayer walks in the cities, praying for my people. And when I meet people in my work, I often have a chance to plant seeds of truth. Please pray for us. Our country needs Jesus."

The grave of another man is also reputed to lie in Samarkand—the biblical prophet, Daniel, a Jewish exile who rose to second in the kingdom during the reign of Babylonian king Nebuchadnezzar and Persian kings Cyrus and Darius the Mede, whose kingdom at one time held sway over what is now Uzbekistan.

In 1941 Soviet anthropologist Mikhail Gerasimov opened the Guri Amir Mausoleum and verified that a large man with injuries to his right leg and arm (suffered when he was twenty-five) lies beneath the splendid aqua dome that came to typify imperial architecture of that era—the "Timurid" style. Everything fit the historical descriptions of Tamerlane.

No one has verified the remains of Daniel purported to have been transported here by Amur Temur, who surrounded himself with artisans, scientists, and holy relics. Yet the tomb holds an enduring mystique. Daniel, an exile from his Jewish homeland in life and perhaps still further in death, is nevertheless truly home in the kingdom he saw prophetically (see Daniel 2) in a way the restless, violent, searching Amur Temur never was.

Alexander the Great, Constantine, Genghis Khan, and Amur Temur are conquerors whose empires have risen and fallen. Their footprints remain in names of cities, rivers, peoples. We pondered the dozens of layers of civilization that have come and gone—plundering, sacking, borrowing, building.

Tamerlane's tomb in Samarkand, Uzbekistan.

Sometimes rulers have favored one religion over another, founding a national religion that shapes national identity. Others, such as the great Kublai Khan, grandson of Genghis Khan, have been surprisingly tolerant, wanting to learn and benefit from the wisdom of all. Coming from a shamanistic Mongol background, Kublai had a Buddhist wife but a Christian mother who was a member of the ancient Church of the East.

Many Christians look with joy on the conversion of Constantine. Persecution of Christians ceased and regal churches like Hagia Sophia in Constantinople (Istanbul) rose. Yet eastern Christian communities in Persia suffered immensely when the rival Roman Empire became Christian.

Before rulers such as Amur Temur consolidated Islam as the unifying religion, a wide variety of religions—Zoroastrianism, shamanism, Buddhism, Christianity, and Judaism—mingled in central Asia like so many spices in the bazaar, all distinct and separate but the aro-

A MIG jet Soviet memorial in Aktau.

mas blending, beckoning. The Silk Road carried Buddhist missionaries north from India, Christian missionaries east from Syria.

Although the early Christian witnesses spoke Syriac and kept their hymns, creeds, liturgies, and Scriptures in that tongue, they did not carry the connection to empire that often tarnished later Portuguese, Spanish, Dutch, and British missionaries. And though these later missionaries regularly dissociated themselves from the greed and exploitation of their colonizing nations, often openly critiquing and challenging national policies, they could not escape the reality of association.

As Christians whose ancestors were also persecuted, banished, and killed in Europe in the sixteenth and seventeenth centuries, we grieved that Christianity has been so frequently identified with the empires of the western world. It seems so unlike Jesus.

Jesus neither sought the endorsement and backing of the power brokers of his day nor treated a ruler with greater dignity and respect than he did a powerless blind beggar. Yet beginning with Constantine, Christianity gradually came to be associated with what became "the West," opening it to the charges of imperialism as western Christian empires sent their merchants and missionaries east.

Christian missionaries such as the Syrian Alopen and the Italian Matteo Ricci were situated high in the imperial courts and sought to influence the Chinese rulers to adopt the Christian faith. But time and again this approach in Asia led to fear, rising nationalism, and waves of persecution that sought to drive Christianity, "the western religion," from the country.

We know that only one heavenly kingdom quietly grows to fill the whole earth. But we cannot escape our identification with some nation of this world too. It's normal, then, that we may be seen as disloyal, as were Daniel and his three friends who refused to worship the king or his golden image. On the other hand, how

An Afghani shoe shiner.

can we avoid the regular identification of Christianity with one or another nation of the world?

In the spring of 2007, three Christians, one a German missionary and two Turkish believers from Muslim backgrounds, died at the hands of young nationalistic Turks in Malatya, Turkey. "To be Turkish is to be Muslim," the murderers insisted. "Christians are insulting Turkishness." But who can fault Muslims for identifying their faith with political power when the same has been done so frequently by Christians?

In central Asia, rising nationalism is causing a reaction against Christianity. To be Christian is to be Russian (or sometimes American). It reminds us of God-and-country, nationalistic Christianity back home.

But central Asian followers of Jesus are persevering. Arrests at a birthday party, friends in prison, and ongoing interrogation and harassment by local officials are a constant concern. But "Jesus never said it would be easy," as a newfound friend said.

Chapter 11

Turkish Civilization and the Ancient Church of Asia

On a sixty-hour train ride across the Kazakh steppes, a young surgeon appeared at our elbow and engaged us in English. He was headed back to work in his hometown and told us we were the first Americans he had ever met.

We were soon deeply engaged in a wide-ranging conversation that took us to Islam, Christianity, Kazakh and American politics, families, and then a probing, challenging question about great world civilizations. "I have read," he said, "that when western historians list the major world civilizations, they do not include the Turkish. Is that correct?"

In a flash, the uncomfortable truth dawned. "You are right," Richard said. "The list of major world civilizations I've used does not include Turkish. But I see after this trip that it should. We are biased."[33]

In Van, Turkey, we bought a Turkish historical atlas designed for students. The very first map outlines the major world civilizations, and the one that has by far the largest geographical range, dominating all Eurasia, is the "central Asian Turkish civilization."[34] Western biases are matched well by Turkish. If Turkish civilization does not appear on western lists, neither does western civilization appear on Turkish lists.

The conversation on the Kazakh train had indeed been a moment of truth. All along the way we had been looking for the intersections between Turkic peoples and the ancient Christian mission to central Asia. Evidence for it was everywhere, yet there was no connected history. Standing on the ruins of the ancient Nestorian church building at Sujab (modern-day Aq-beshim) in the Chuy Valley east of Bishkek, we saw that there within the walls of a tenth-century Karakhanid Turkish city had been a Christian place of worship for central Asians. But apart from the ruins, the crosses, and a few graveyard inscriptions from the region, there was little to be learned.

On the other hand, the western bias against the Turks seemed to be illustrated even in the history we were reading.[35] They seemed

A typical covered bazaar in central Asia.

The old Silk Road is remembered with banners and signs.

always to be found on the margins of the larger, more important movements of peoples and nations. The Chinese, Persians, and Russians were usually the major players.

The Turkish people are the ethnic anchor of central Asia, with enormous, significant intersections both west and east. On our Silk Road pilgrimage, perhaps nothing illustrated this better than the story of Sorkaktani.[36]

Around the year 1000, the Kerait Turks of central Asia became Christians. This was said to have taken place as a result of a vision the Kerait king had while hopelessly lost in the high mountains. A saint appeared to him and said, "If you believe in Christ, I will lead you lest you perish."[37]

The king returned safely, and later he met some Christian merchants who in turn sent him to the archbishop of Merv, in the land between the rivers. Two hundred thousand of the Kerait tribe were baptized.

For the next two hundred years, the Kerait Turks were known as Christians. They became the first of the Turkic tribes to befriend

A visit to Urartian ruins in Van, Turkey.

Yesugei, a petty chieftain of an insignificant subclan—but the father of Genghis Khan.

Genghis, in turn, defeated the Kerait Turks when he suspected them of treachery, but he married the oldest daughter of a brother of the fallen chief. Her younger sister he gave as a wife to his oldest son, and the third daughter, Sorkaktani, he gave in marriage to his fourth son, Tolui. Thus there were three Christian Turkish sisters married to khans of the great Mongol Empire. Genghis obviously respected the Keraits.

Sorkaktani became famous both for her devotion as a Christian and her administrative ability. Her husband, a brilliant general, died when he was only forty-two, leaving her with four young sons. She refused remarriage in order to give her full attention to educating her sons.

Her sons, in turn, entered the annals of global civilizations as some of the greatest military and political leaders in history. Her second son was Kublai Khan, who ruled the great Mongol Empire at its height (1260-1294), overseeing the Pax Mongolica that covered nearly all of Asia, except some peninsular border areas such as western Europe, parts of India, and a bit of southeast Asia.

Sorkaktani's first son, Mongke, served as a Great Khan of the empire preceding Kublai, and her third son, Hulegu, ruled the southeastern portion of the empire from Persia during the reign of Kublai, his older brother. Arikbuka, the fourth son, was more strongly drawn to his mother's Christianity than any of the others, but he lost the succession to the throne in civil war with Kublai.

As we traveled through central Asia, we pondered the influence of Sorkaktani and the Kerait Turks. Sorkaktani had ruled so wisely and well that sixty years after her death she was proclaimed empress of the whole empire.[38] Almost certainly as a direct result of his mother's influence, Kublai Khan was both a highly accomplished administrator of the world's largest empire to date and a generous, sympathetic supporter of Asian Christianity.

In Kublai's time, trade between east and west was brisk along the old Silk Road. Through the Polo brothers, he sent an urgent appeal in 1270 asking the pope to send one hundred learned Christians to China to instruct them in the truth of the Christian faith.[39] He did this, he said, because in his day the Christianity of the Church of the

Turkish school children with Mount Ararat in the background.

East in China was too morally and intellectually weak to stand against the spiritual powers of Tibetan Buddhism. Yet he himself believed that Christianity was the true religion, and he wanted to be converted.

We'll never be able to answer the "what ifs" of Christianity in Asia. It now appears that Chinese civilization, the longest-lasting and most durable in history, has for millennia maintained a posture of respect and honor for the creator God very close to that of the Hebrews and Christians themselves.[40]

Did the ancient Syrian and Persian evangelists to China fail to grasp the intrinsic openness of the Chinese people to the creator God who came to us in Jesus? Did Christianity remain too foreign in all its presentations, including those of Turkic Christians at the time of Sorkaktani, many centuries later? Did the western church experience one of its greatest missionary failures at the time of Kublai Khan's unanswered request for one hundred learned Christians?

And what of the great movements to Jesus in China today? Has the faithfulness of Xavier, Ricci, Hudson Taylor and a myriad of other western Christian witnesses in the past five hundred years resulted in a Chinese embrace of Jesus that connects the ancient Chinese reverence for the creator God with the good news of salvation through Christ more fully than ever before? Brother Yun and Peter Xu, Chinese house-church leaders, obviously think so.

And the Turks? Is that great Turkic civilization binding all of central Asia in one great clasp from Xian to Istanbul also on the verge of reopening its doors to the faith of Sorkaktani? The radiant Kyrgyz pastor and our young friends from a neighboring country think so. Far to the west in the western Turkic world, there are others who think so too.

Everywhere we went, we saw "clouds the size of a man's hand" on the horizon. In China, the rain has begun. In central and west Asia, the cloud is growing.

Chapter 12

Opposition and Persecution

We sat on the floor, enjoying a late-evening meal of chicken, rice pilaf, and salad with a western Turkic pastor, his wife, and five children. We laughed and reminisced together. Then his face grew sober. "I've been told that I'm high on the hit list," he said. "Three of our Christian brothers were martyred last spring. Nothing like this has happened in recent history. Did you hear that private investigators of those deaths uncovered evidence that the five young men who killed the Christians had connections to the police and high government officials? I don't know how long I have to live, but my life is in God's hands."

∞

"The blood of the martyrs is the seed of the church," wrote Tertullian.

One day in 1988 we got an unexpected call from a young man we'd left in charge of a small house church in the western Asian nation from which we'd been deported earlier.

"I just heard that the police are on their way to arrest me. Please pray," he said. Then the line went dead.

The next morning, with tears, we read from John 15 and 16, "Don't be surprised at the fiery trials. . . . If they persecuted me, they will persecute you."

As we prayed for dear brothers and sisters in Christ, we wondered what they would be asked to suffer for Jesus' sake. Would they stand firm? Would the tiny, vulnerable house church be snuffed out?

We remembered our Anabaptist ancestors, who were zealous for God in sixteenth-century Germany, Holland, Switzerland, France, and Austria. Imprisoned or banished to farm only above a thousand meters in the Alps, many were hounded to extinction by shoot-on-sight "Baptist hunters" in Austria. Many fled to the New World, which offered freedom from state churches intolerant of dissent. Weary and wounded, they settled in America, where they became more known for tidy, prosperous farms than for fearless evangelism.

The Anabaptist movement helped to seed the evangelical movement, which has flung missionaries around the world, but North American Mennonite communities did not officially send their first foreign missionaries until 1899, almost one hundred years after the first American foreign missionaries to Asia, Adoniram and Ann Judson, sailed for Burma in 1810. But the persecution suffered by those Anabaptists is only a tiny fraction of the persecution suffered by faithful Christians through the centuries.

In west, central, and east Asia, hostile governments have stifled, oppressed, and in some cases completely wiped out the once-populous Church of the East, with its large mission training centers in Edessa and Nisibis. Remnants of the church in its various communions now live in tiny ethnic enclaves in eastern Turkey, Syria, Iraq, Iran, Lebanon, Israel/Palestine, and Jordan. Except for Russia to the north and the Philippines in the far east, Armenia and Georgia are the only Asian nations where Christianity is the dominant faith.

Today it is hard to believe that hundreds of missionaries streamed from these churches, laying down their lives to evangelize all across the steppes of central Asia and on into Mongolia, India, and China.

Near the end of our trip, we participated in evening prayers at the Dayrul Zarayan Monastery in Mardin, Turkey, headquarters for a community of about three thousand Christians of the regional Apostolic Syrian Orthodox Church. We learned that the oldest part of the monastery dates back to the third century and was built by missionaries from Edessa, who planted the church and built atop a pagan worship site that is still visible.

While the church stewards a precious history and liturgy that stretches back to the apostolic era, it is no longer reproducing. Like the Mennonite descendants of the European Anabaptists did for many years, it has hunkered down to survive. Centuries of taxation

Carpets bearing the "Golgotha motif" of three crosses on a hill are still woven by Turkmen villagers who have long forgotten their Christian roots.

Hayriye, a Bulgarian Turkish pastor's wife, cooked a sumptuous chicken dinner in her outdoor kitchen during the dead of winter.

and minority status within the context of various governments have led to steady decline and migration to the West, where there are more opportunities for education and employment.

On a Sunday morning in southeastern Turkey, we worshipped at the evangelical church, across the street from the second-century Syrian Church of the Virgin Mary. The Turkish pastor and the flock of sixty to seventy believers open their doors to any who wish to come.

"We always invite the Syrian Christians to our special events," the pastor said as his congregation distributed invitations to a Christmas program the following week. "But they don't reach out. You have to be Syrian to attend their church. When local people come to their church with questions about Jesus, they send them to us. They're happy to see their neighbors interested in Jesus, but they do not have a vision to include them in their church."

In contrast, the Syrian congregation next door has dwindled to about two families. The community of seventy Syrian families in Mardin, sixty miles away, rotates their worship services among seven different church buildings that they are trying to maintain as "active."

"Here in the Middle East they say that 'religion is in the blood,'" an American friend commented. "It's very difficult for traditional Middle Eastern Christians to accept Muslim-background believers into their congregations. It's all too easy to have one's religion defined by one's ethnicity."

The great persecutions of the Persian Church of the East between 339 and 401 led to the deaths of as many as 190,000 believers. This persecution under the Persians was far worse than anything suffered in the West under Rome, yet the number of apostasies was fewer.[41]

When these persecutions began, Bishop Simon was told that if only he would apostasize, his people would not be harmed. But if he refused, he would be condemning not just the church leaders but all Christians to destruction. Upon hearing this, the church rose up and refused to accept such a shameful deliverance. So on Good Friday 344, five bishops and one hundred priests were beheaded, and in the following decades Christians were tracked down and hunted from one end of the empire to the other.[42]

Further north and east of Mardin lies the new country of Armenia. A small nation of three million, recently independent of the Soviet Union, it is struggling to rebuild in the plains and mountains east of Mount Ararat. The earliest "Christian" nation, they have "kept the faith" since 301 through incredible suffering and dislocation.

And just to its north is Georgia, on the southern edge of the Caucasus Mountains—another "Christian" country since the fifth century, when St. Nino's prayers saved the life of the queen and led to the conversion of the royal household, then the kingdom. Yet along with the Armenians, there is hardly a people that has been more battered by neighboring empires.

So, on one level, this sampling of Asian Christian history seems to give the lie to Tertullian's words about the blood of the martyrs. On the contrary, persecution seems to have almost stamped out the church in Turkey, Japan, Iran, and Iraq, and across central Asia.

Yet the reality is not so simple. The times of greatest persecution did not destroy the ancient Asian church. On the contrary, the rapid expansion of the church came during and after some of the harshest persecutions. It was only after the church had withdrawn into a traditional survival mode that it began to be choked out by vigorous religious alternatives. And precisely when these seem doomed to extinction, other dynamic forms of Christian witness move back in with the old spiritual fire.

Why? The church of Jesus Christ cannot be contained in any one catholicos. Earthly ecclesiastical authorities—many with direct apostolic connections like the Mar Thoma Church of India (apostle Thomas), the Armenian and Georgian Apostolic Churches (apostles Bartholomew and Thaddeus), the Roman Catholic Church (the apostle Peter), the Greek Orthodox Church (the apostles Peter and Paul), the Egyptian Coptic Church (the apostle Mark), the Apostolic Syrian Orthodox Church (the apostle Addai)—have maintained a faithful core while being pushed into narrow ethnic enclaves to survive.

But even as the fires of faith are smothered or squelched in one location, the sparks fly elsewhere to light a fire. For example, our joy in witnessing the growth of the church today in places like Indonesia, Peru, or Vietnam comes from seeing that the Anabaptist fires of the sixteenth century helped lay the spiritual foundations for the powerful evangelical movements in Europe and North America that resulted in the modern missionary movement, ignit-

Mount Ararat.

ing new spiritual fires in places like Honduras, Kenya, and Korea. The movement continues.

When Richard was interrogated by local western Turkic authorities in 1986, they found it impossible to understand what had brought us to a mundane, industrial, gray city far from home. Surely we must be receiving large monetary rewards from the U.S. government.

"They don't understand spiritual motivation," we mused. "They don't know the unparalleled joy of seeing new brothers and sisters becoming part of the body of Christ." Here is something priceless, something worth dying for.

With joy, believers have laid down their lives for the greatest cause on earth. "For me, to live is Christ, to die is gain," wrote the apostle Paul. Gain for the kingdom. The grain is buried in the ground, dead, but, like Jesus, springing up into new multiplied kernels. Yes, Tertullian, the blood of the martyrs is still the seed of the church.

Chapter 13

Why Did the Church Disappear?

"This mosque used to be a church," our friend pointed out. "You can tell by the way it's laid out. There were hundreds of Christian churches and schools in eastern Turkey that have been put to other uses since that large Christian community was displaced in 1915. The Syrian Orthodox community here in the southeast is trying desperately to hold on to their buildings, but their population is shrinking. In one city they're rotating their small group of worshippers between seven different buildings to show they are all still actively in use."

We joined evening mass at the Syrian Orthodox Zarayan Monastery outside Mardin. Young boys joined the monks in chanting the ancient liturgies compiled from the Syriac scriptures and writings of the church fathers. We did not understand a word of what was said. We weren't sure the young lads did either, but they were carrying on a centuries-old tradition that has sustained their ancestors and once sent missionaries all the way to India and China.

Why did the church disappear in so many parts of Asia?

At the fortress in Sujab, an ancient Turkish city, once a Christian center, near Bishkek, Kyrgyzstan.

No other question has been put to us more often. Sometimes it's when we lead tours of the sites of the "seven churches of Revelation" in western Turkey. We visit the ruins of the ancient cities of the Roman Empire where the churches to which John wrote once worshipped, but now there's nothing obvious remaining. Why the change? Why the absence today?

Now, too, as we share our excitement about the great missionary movement of the Church of the East eastward in the first thousand years of Christian history, the question is repeated constantly: "So there was once a church in Balkh, Afghanistan, from which witnesses were sent all the way to the capital of China. Why no longer?"

The question is serious, insistent. It deserves an answer. Or rather, it deserves a probing, thoughtful response, for the most apparent answers are often misleading.

The most common answer is that "Islam wiped out the church. There was once a thriving church, but Muslims came with the sword and an alternative religion and sometimes quickly, sometimes gradually, they replaced the church by overt or covert force."

The western scholarly elite give this answer as frequently as do local church leaders and members. It is appealing, because it seems to account so well for so many of the facts.

It is true that in North Africa, the Middle East, and central Asia, there were once flourishing Christian churches, and today all these regions are largely Islamic. It is true that in the Islamic community the governmental sword and the "true religion" (Islam) go hand in hand. It cannot be denied that the sword has often been used to advance the Islamic community or that by taking away key "rights" of traditional Christian populations, Muslim leaders initiated a subtle, centuries-long coercion away from Christianity toward the Muslim faith.

Appealing though it is, however, this answer is unsatisfactory. We observe that it is often given by Christians who stand in traditions in

Enjoying a meal with a Turkish pastor and his family in Burgas, Bulgaria.

which they too have used the sword to promote the faith. It leads to positing a great power struggle between Islam and Christianity in which it is important to secure the borders of "Christian nations" by the same means that "Muslim nations" use. If only Persia or central Asia had had a Constantine!

But that is not the way of Jesus. True, a "Christian ruler" may help ensure the continuation of a particular traditional form of Christianity. This was the experience of the church in Europe for many centuries. It is also our experience in the United States, in a somewhat different form. Yet these "western Christian governments" have often taken positions that throttled vibrant forms of the very Christianity they espoused, as with the radical reformation of sixteenth-century Europe.

So, if Constantine is the answer, Jesus is not. If it is dependent on earthly political power for its existence, Jesus' way of the cross and suffering love is inherently and deeply compromised.

Furthermore, as we have already noted, the periods of harshest persecution of the church did not result in its extinction. Rather, in those periods it usually continued to grow—often even more rapidly than in times of peace. Arguably, the most severe persecution of the Christian church in all of its history took place in fifth-century Zoroastrian Persia, before Islam even existed. Yet the church continued to flourish then and for centuries after. In fact, about that time it began one of its greatest seasons of missionary expansion eastward.

So why did it eventually disappear in so many places? Another answer is that it disappeared because it was not orthodox in theology. Western Christians have long given this answer about the Church of the East. After all, it was declared heretical by the church of the West in the sixth century and given the name *Nestorian*. A church that is not orthodox will die. We in the West were orthodox; they in the East were not.

Christians in the western stream (including Roman Catholic

A view of Herat, Afghanistan, from inside an ancient fortress dating to the time of Abraham.

and Protestants) have also often given this answer about the disappearance of many Eastern Orthodox churches in western Asia. The seven churches of Asia Minor to which the apostle John wrote in Revelation were Eastern Orthodox churches. They were close to us in faith, but not quite close enough!

However, this answer also does not withstand careful examination. The more we have learned about both the Church of the East and the Eastern Orthodox, the less ready we are to dub them heretics. In fact, when evangelical missionaries first encountered the Church of the East in the nineteenth century, they found them so much like Protestants in theology that they quickly embraced them as long-lost brothers. And today's evangelical youth in North America are drawn in increasing numbers to the Eastern Orthodox communion as a solid bastion of true orthodoxy.

After traveling the Silk Road, we think there is a better answer:

The church finally disappears when it no longer has the vitality to evangelize its enemies and neighbors. Theoretically, heavy persecution can eliminate the church. Sometimes it seems to do so for a season. But the forgiving love of Christ is powerful beyond words. When brothers and sisters forgive their enemies while continuing to proclaim the good news, the message of salvation and deliverance in Jesus will never be finally and fully repressed. God will see to that. Remember Candida, the Christian wife of the Zoroastrian shah of Persia.

On the other hand, whatever "church" endures without that forgiving love of Christ is not worthy of the name.

Jesus walked it out all the way to the cross and beyond. The power of the risen Christ springs up in resurrection glory, not only for himself but also for his body, the church. That resurrection life is still to be seen today all along the path from Xian to Istanbul. We saw it and rejoiced.

Finally, let's never judge any church because it "disappeared." It is quite possible that a church that lived through seasons of tremendous opposition and brokenness due to external pressures and persecution will prove one day to have been stronger than another that seemed to have lasted much longer and endured by dependence on political power and wealth. God forbid that the West should judge the East.

We remember too that each human generation has its life to live. What matters is not the historical longevity of institutions but the vitality of life and witness while we live.

So we celebrate the Church of the East in both its ancient and modern expressions. Kingdom traffic along the Silk Road has never halted.

Notes

1. Marco Polo, *Travels of Marco Polo* (Baltimore: Penguin, 1958), 235-7.

2. The Nestorian Tablet was carved in Chinese and Syriac in 781 and details the coming of Christianity to the T'ang Dynasty court in 635. The original is housed in a Xian museum. An ancient Christian pagoda dating from the T'ang Dynasty still stands, though leaning dangerously, near Xian. Scrolls written by Chinese and central Asian Christians were discovered at the ancient library of the Mogao Grottoes near Dunhuang in 1907 by Aurel Stein, a Hungarian-born archaeologist working for the British government in India. The library had been sealed up for almost a thousand years and had recently been rediscovered as a result of an earthquake. The foundations of a thousand-year-old Church of the East church building in the ruins of the Karakhanid Turkish city of Sujab near the modern village of Aq-beshim in the Chuy Valley, east of Bishkek, have recently been identified. Other evidences are too numerous to mention here. See especially John C. England, *The Hidden History of Christianity in Asia* (Delhi: Indian Society for Promoting Christian Knowledge, 1996) for further details.

3. Brother Yun's story is told in Brother Yun with Paul Hattaway, *The Heavenly Man: The Remarkable True Story of Brother Yun* (Grand Rapids, Mich.: Kregel, 2002). Further information on the Back to Jerusalem movement among Chinese house churches can be found in Paul Hattaway, *Back to Jerusalem: Three Chinese House Church Leaders*

Share Their Vision to Complete the Great Commission, (Carlisle, U.K.: Piquant, Gabriel Resources, 2003). The meeting in Bechterdissen, Germany, was the 2007 annual meeting of the International Missions Association, a group of Anabaptist mission leaders representing groups of churches in Asia, Africa, Latin America, and North America.

4. England, 43.

5. Ibid., 136, 151.

6. While traveling the Silk Road, we read Samuel Hugh Moffett's two-volume *A History of Christianity in Asia* (Maryknoll, N.Y.: Orbis, 1998, 2005). We also read *Travels of Marco Polo* (London: Penguin Classics, 1958), translated by Ronald Latham on the basis of early four-teenth-century French and Italian texts—a remarkable, firsthand depiction by a medieval European of the thirteenth-century world of the Pax Mongolica overseen by Kublai Khan of China's Yuan Dynasty, the most extensive empire Eurasia has ever known, encompassing essentially the whole landmass except the peninsulas of Europe, India, Arabia, and parts of the south-east Asia peninsula.

7. See the map of the Silk Road on page 8.

8. Moffett, vol. 1, 32-36.

9. Ibid., 112.

10. Ibid. Her name was Candida (Qndyr), and the date of martyr-dom was probably between AD 286 and 291 (115).

11. Ibid., 78, 79; also 47.

12. Ibid., 79, 207. The ancient name of this region was Bactria.

13. Ibid., 300. The T'ang Dynasty name for Xian was Chang'an.

14. Ibid., 207-9.

15. Moffett, vol. 2, 108-11.

16. The Reformation was really a renewal of the whole church of the West, including the new Protestants, the Roman Catholics, and the Anabaptists. It is unfortunate that the term "Protestant Reformation" is so universally used to describe it.

17. Moffett, vol. 2, 9-11.

18. Moffett, vol. 1, 200-3.

19. Ibid., 78-9.

20. J. C. Pollock, *Hudson Taylor and Maria: Pioneers in China*, (Bromley, U.K.: Kingsway, 1983), 9-10.

21. See Romans 16:5; 1 Corinthians 16:19; Colossians 4:15; Philemon 2. See also Acts 2:46; Philippians 4:22.

22. Moffett, vol. 1, 93.

23. See Nathan Hege, *Beyond Our Prayers* (Scottdale, Pa.: Herald Press, 1998). When the socialist government of Ethiopia officially closed the Meserete Kristos Church in 1982, the congregation changed to the house-church pattern. In spite of, or perhaps because of, this change, the church grew from 4,500 members in 1982 to more than 30,000 in 1991, when the church was opened again. It continued to grow rapidly but still maintains the house fellowships. As of 2008, the Meserete Kristos Church is the world's largest Anabaptist ecclesiastical union, with more than 150,000 baptized members. In Amharic, see Tilahun Beyene Kidane.

24. Hattaway, *Back to Jerusalem*, 92-4.

25. Moffett, vol. 2, 502.

26. Ibid., 503.

27. Moffett, vol. 1, 314.

28. See, for example, Polo, *Travels*.

29. Gene Daniels, *Seen in a Different Light: A Local Perspective on Missionaries in Kyrgyzstan*, unpublished manuscript, copyright 2007 by Gene Daniels (pseud.).

30. In missiological terms, "adaptation" is often called "contextualization." Deciding about faithfulness and unfaithfulness of doctrine is often discussed in terms of "syncretism."

31. Daniels, *passim*.

32. Moffett, vol. 1, 207-9.

33. See Samuel P. Huntington, *The Clash of Civilizations and the Remaking of World Order* (New York: Simon & Schuster, 1996), 40-48. The major contemporary civilizations, according to Huntington, and on which "reasonable agreement" exists among scholars are Sinic (Chinese),

Japanese, Hindu, Islamic, Orthodox, Western, Latin American, and (possibly) African. Seven that no longer exist are Mesopotamian, Egyptian, Cretan, Classical, Byzantine, Middle American, and Andean. Arab, Turkic, Persian, and Malay are recognized as "subcivilizations" within the Islamic whole (45). However, if this sub-classification pattern is used for Islam, it would seem to make equal sense to use it for Christianity, referring to a "Christian" or "western" civilization with sub-civilizations designated as Orthodox and Latin American. Huntington's western bias is obvious.

34. Adnan Cinar and Funda Cinar, *Tarih Atlasi* (Ankara: Tashkin Yayincilik, n.d.), 5. This atlas lists major world civilizations throughout history and is fascinating when placed alongside Huntington's list. It identifies the Aztec, Mayan, Incan, Hittite, Egyptian, Phoenician, Greek, Roman, Byzantine, Sumerian, Akkadian, Chaldean, Assyrian, Babylonian, Iranian, Hindu, and Chinese civilizations along with the central Asian Turkish. While it is not entirely fair to compare a scholarly list with one found in a school atlas, the differences between a Turkish and a western perspective on major world civilizations are striking.

35. See especially Moffett, vol. 1, 380, 384-5, 387; Moffett, vol. 2, 382. There are, of course, obvious, if not compelling, reasons for the bad press in the West. With names like Attila the Hun, Genghis Khan, and Tamerlane adorning their historical interactions with European civilization, it is not surprising that the Mongol-Turkic peoples of central and east Asia have not been warmly embraced in the West. The West returned the favor with the medieval Crusades.

36. Moffett, vol. 1, 402, 443-5.

37. Ibid., 400.

38. Ibid., 443.

39. Polo, 120.

40. Chan Kei Thong, *Faith of our Fathers: God in Ancient China* (Shanghai: Orient Publishing Center, 2006).

41. Moffett, vol. 1, 145.

42. Ibid., 140.

The Authors

Richard and Jewel Showalter are both associated with Eastern Mennonite Missions. Richard became president in 1994, and Jewel has been a staff writer and representative to the Middle East and North Africa since 2000. They served from 1982 to 1989 in western Asia with Rosedale Mennonite Missions. Both have written extensively for Mennonite and other periodicals and journals. Richard is the author of *On the Way with Jesus: A Passion for Mission* (Herald Press, 2008), and Jewel is co-author with Elmer Yoder of *We Beheld His Glory: A History of Rosedale Bible Institute* (1992). They live in Landisville, Pennsylvania, and are members of West End Mennonite Fellowship in Lancaster, Pennsylvania.